PowerPoint Essentials 2019

M.L. HUMPHREY

ISBN: 978-1-63744-067-4

SELECT TITLES BY M.L. HUMPHREY

POWERPOINT ESSENTIALS 2019

PowerPoint 2019 Beginner

PowerPoint 2019 Intermediate

EXCEL ESSENTIALS 2019

Excel 2019 Beginner

Excel 2019 Intermediate

Excel 2019 Formulas & Functions

WORD ESSENTIALS 2019

Word 2019 Beginner

Word 2019 Intermediate

ACCESS ESSENTIALS 2019

Access 2019 Beginner

Access 2019 Intermediate

CONTENTS

PowerPoint 2019 Beginner

POWERPOINT ESSENTIALS 2019 BOOK 1

M.L. HUMPHREY

CONTENTS

CONTENTS (CONT.)

Introduction

This guide focuses specifically on how to use Microsoft PowerPoint 2019. If you have an older version of PowerPoint, *PowerPoint for Beginners*, the predecessor to this book, is likely a better choice because it was written to be more generic and accessible to users of any version of PowerPoint from 2007 onward.

This guide, *PowerPoint 2019 Beginner*, just focuses on how to use Microsoft PowerPoint 2019. What that means, practically speaking, is that all screenshots in this book will be from PowerPoint 2019 and all instructions in this book will be written for users of PowerPoint 2019.

At the beginner level there really isn't a significant difference between the two books and you will likely be able to use either one to learn PowerPoint. You definitely do not need both of them.

Alright, then. Now that we have that out of the way.

The purpose of this guide is to introduce you to the basics of using Microsoft PowerPoint 2019, which is one of the go-to software programs for creating presentation slides. I've used it throughout my professional career and I know of a number of students who have also needed to use it for class presentations.

It is a fantastic tool, but if you've ever been on the receiving end of a consulting presentation, you likely also know how it can be misused by people who cram far too much information into a single slide for it to actually work as a presentation.

Same goes for if you've ever been subjected to someone who got a little too excited about the bells and whistles available through PowerPoint and created a presentation where every single page or bullet point whizzed and spun and danced onto the screen.

(As you can tell, I have opinions about proper presentations. To me a presentation should give enough information to prompt the speaker to remember what they need to say, but not be such a distraction that no one listens to the speaker. You want to write a report? Write a report. You want to have dancing, spinning, spiraling text? You better be in third grade.)

Anyway. PowerPoint is a useful and important program to learn. The goal for this book is to teach you enough of it that you can comfortably use one of the PowerPoint templates to create your own presentation which includes text, pictures, and/or tables of information.

You will also learn how to format any text you enter, how to add notes to your slides, how to animate your slides so that each bullet point appears separately, and how to launch your presentation as a slide show. We will also cover how to print a copy of your presentation as well as how to print handouts.

As you can see, I will also be sprinkling in my opinion throughout this guide so it isn't just going to be how to do things in PowerPoint but why you might want to do it in a certain way.

There are other aspects to PowerPoint that I'm not going to cover in this guide. For example, we're not going to discuss how to use SmartArt. Nor will we discuss how to insert charts or create a presentation from scratch. If you want to continue with your knowledge of PowerPoint, many of those topics are covered in *PowerPoint 2019 Intermediate*.

The goal of this guide is to give you enough information on how to create a basic presentation without overwhelming you with information you may not need. I will, however, end with a discussion of how to find help for any additional topics you need to learn. PowerPoint, just like Word and Excel, has a certain underlying logic to it and if you pay attention to that structure it's generally easy to find what you need when you need it.

There is definitely overlap between how things work in Word and Excel, so if you've already mastered one of those programs PowerPoint will be much easier for you to learn. But if you haven't, we'll cover what you need to know, don't worry.

Alright then. First things first, let's get started with some basic terminology.

Basic Terminology

Before we do anything else, I want to make sure that we're on the same page in terms of terminology. Some of this will be standard to anyone talking about these programs and some of it is my personal quirky way of saying things, so best to skim through if nothing else.

Tab

I refer to the menu choices at the top of the screen (File, Home, Insert, Design, Transitions, Animations, Slide Show, Review, View, etc.) as tabs. If you click on one you'll see that the way it's highlighted sort of looks like an old-time filing system.

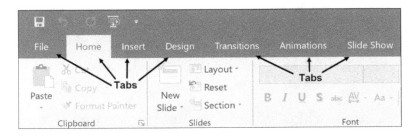

Each tab you select will show you different options. For example, in the image above, I have the Home tab selected and you can do various tasks such as cut/copy/paste, add new slides, change the slide layout, change fonts or font size or font color, change text formatting, add shapes, find/replace, etc. Other tabs will give other options.

Click

If I tell you to click on something, that means to use your mouse (or trackpad) to move the arrow on the screen over to a specific location and left-click or right-click on the option. (See the next definition for the difference between left-click and right-click).

If you left-click, this selects the item. If you right-click, this generally creates a dropdown list of options to choose from. If I don't tell you which to do, left- or right-click, then left-click.

Left-Click/Right-Click

If you look at your mouse or your trackpad, you generally have two flat buttons to press. One is on the left side, one is on the right. If I say left-click that means to press down on the button on the left. If I say right-click that means press down on the button on the right.

Now, as I sadly learned when I had to upgrade computers, not all trackpads have the left- and right-hand buttons. In that case, you'll basically want to press on either the bottom left-hand side of the trackpad or the bottom right-hand side of the trackpad. Since you're working blind it may take a little trial and error to get the option you want working. (Or is that just me?)

Select or Highlight

If I tell you to select text, that means to left-click at the end of the text you want to select, hold that left-click, and move your cursor to the other end of the text you want to select.

Another option is to use the Shift key. Go to one end of the text you want to select. Hold down the shift key and use the arrow keys to move to the other end of the text you want to select. If you arrow up or down, that will select an entire row at a time.

With both methods, which side of the text you start on doesn't matter. You can start at the end and go to the beginning or start at the beginning and go to the end. Just start at one end or the other of the text you want to select.

The text you've selected will then be highlighted in gray.

If you need to select text that isn't touching you can do this by selecting your first section of text and then holding down the Ctrl key and selecting your second section of text using your mouse.

(You can't arrow to the second section of text or you'll lose your already selected text.)

To select an object, you can generally just left-click on it. To select multiple objects, hold down the Ctrl key as you click on each object.

To select everything in your workspace, you can use Ctrl + A. (This is a control shortcut, which we'll define in a moment.)

Dropdown Menu

If you right-click on a PowerPoint slide, you will see what I'm going to refer to as a dropdown menu. (Sometimes it will actually drop upward if you're towards the bottom of the document.)

A dropdown menu provides you a list of choices to select from like this one that appears when I right-click on a presentation slide:

There are also dropdown menus available for some of the options listed under the tabs at the top of the screen. For example, if you go to the Home tab, you'll see small arrows below or next to some of the options, like the Layout option and the Section option in the Slides section. Clicking on those little arrows will give you a dropdown menu with a list of choices to choose from like this one for Section:

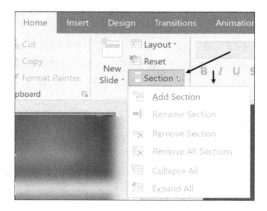

Expansion Arrows

I don't know the official word for these, but you'll also notice at the bottom right corner of most of the sections in each tab that there are little arrows pointing down and to the right.

If you click on one of those arrows PowerPoint will bring up a more detailed set of options, usually through a dialogue box (which we'll discuss next) or a task pane (which we'll discuss after that).

In the Home tab, for example, there are expansion arrows for Clipboard, Font, Paragraph, and Drawing. Holding your mouse over the arrow will give a brief description of what clicking on the expansion arrow will do like here for the Clipboard section on the Home tab where it tells you that clicking on the expansion arrow will allow you to see all items that have been copied to the clipboard.

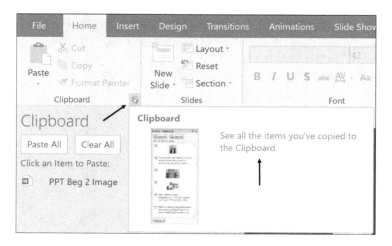

In this instance, clicking on the expansion arrow opens a task pane on the left-hand side of the screen, which is visible in the background of the image above.

Dialogue Box

Dialogue boxes are pop-up boxes that cover specialized settings. As just mentioned, if you click on an expansion arrow, it will often open a dialogue box that contains more choices than are visible in that section.

Also, if you right-click on the text in a PowerPoint content slide and choose Font, Paragraph, or Hyperlink from the dropdown menu that will open a dialogue box.

Dialogue boxes often allow the most granular level of control over an option. For example, this is the Font dialogue box which you can see has more options available than in the Font section of the Home tab.

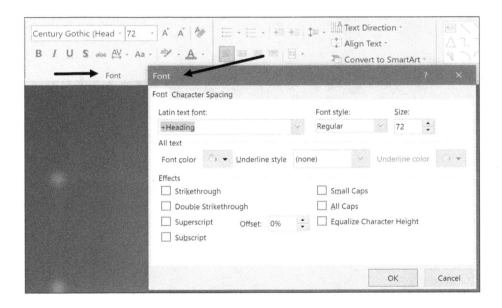

Task Pane

What I refer to as task panes are separate work spaces that are visible to the left- and right-hand sides of your main workspace. They may also occasionally appear below your main workspace.

For example, When you first open PowerPoint, there will generally be a task pane on the left-hand side that shows thumbnail images of the slides in your presentation. This is an area you can navigate in separate from your main workspace.

Here is an example of a business presentation template I opened with the slides in a task pane to the left and the title slide in the main workspace:

You can have multiple task panes open at once. To close a task pane that is not permanently visible, such as the Clipboard task pane, click on the X in the top right corner.

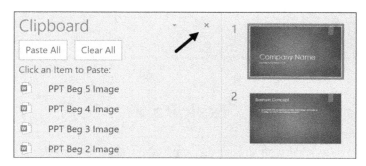

You can also click on the arrow next to the X and choose Close.

You can sometimes also move a task pane. To do so, click on the arrow in the top right corner and choose Move from the dropdown menu. That will detach the task pane from its current position. You can then left-click and drag the task pane to where you'd like.

To attach a task pane to the left-hand or right-hand side of the workspace, drag it off of the edge of the screen until it "docks" into place.

If you do move a task pane and then close it, when you reopen the task pane it will appear in the location you moved it to.

Scroll Bar

Scroll bars allow you to see content that isn't currently visible on the screen. PowerPoint usually has multiple scroll bars visible.

One scroll bar will appear on the right-hand side of the task pane that contains thumbnails of your presentation slides. This scroll bar lets you see the thumbnails of all available slides in the presentation by scrolling up and down.

Here is the top portion of that scroll bar:

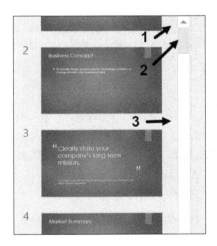

You can click on the up arrow (labeled 1) at the top or the down arrow (not visible here) at the bottom to move a small amount up or down.

If you click on the gray space above or below the scroll bar (labeled 2) that will move you one whole screen at a time. So if Slides 1 through 6 are currently visible, clicking below the scroll bar will make Slides 7 through 12 visible.

Or you can left-click on the scroll bar itself (labeled 3) and drag up or down to move through the available space at your own speed.

I personally tend to left-click and drag the scroll bar because that gives me the most control while still moving through my available slides at a relatively fast pace.

Another scroll bar will generally appear on the right-hand side of the main workspace. This scrollbar will by default let you navigate through each of the slides in your presentation one-by-one.

In the main workspace, there are a few more options. At the bottom of the scroll bar, you have a double up arrow and a double down arrow which can be clicked on to move to the previous slide or the next slide.

When you're at a normal zoom level, you will get that same result by clicking on the gray space above or below the scroll bar or on the arrows at the top or bottom of the scroll bar.

(If you increase the zoom level on your main workspace the scroll bar will instead move through portions of your slides.)

Generally, I don't use the scroll bar for the main workspace because I click onto the thumbnails in the left-hand task pane to move to the slide I want. Or to see an entire presentation one slide at a time I go into Slide Show mode, which we'll discuss later.

You won't normally see a scroll bar at the bottom of the screen, but it is possible. This would happen if you ever change the zoom level to the point that you're not seeing the entire presentation slide on the screen.

Arrow

If I ever tell you to arrow to the left or right or up or down, that just means use your arrow keys. This will move your cursor to the left one space, to the right one space, up one line, or down one line. If you're at the end of a line and arrow to the right, it will take you to the beginning of the next line. If you're at the beginning of a line and arrow to the left, it will take you to the end of the last line.

Cursor

There are two possible meanings for cursor. One is the one I just used. When you're clicked into a PowerPoint slide, you will see that there is a blinking line. This indicates where you are in the document. If you type text, each letter will appear where the cursor was at the time you typed it. The cursor will move (at least in the U.S. and I'd assume most European versions) to the right as you type. This version of the cursor should be visible at all times when you're clicked onto text.

The other type of cursor is the one that's tied to the movement of your mouse or trackpad. If you've clicked onto your text, the cursor will look somewhat like a tall skinny capital I when positioned over text. Move it up to the menu options or off to the sides, and it will generally become a white arrow or four-sided black arrow.

Usually I won't refer to your cursor, I'll just say, "click" or "select" or whatever action you need to take with it, and moving the cursor to that location will be implied.

Quick Access Toolbar

In the very top left corner of your screen above the Home tab, you should see a series of symbols. These are part of the Quick Access Toolbar. By default it appears to have options for Save, Undo, Redo, and Start from Beginning.

To see what each symbol stands for, hold your mouse over it and help text will appear.

You can customize what options appear there by clicking on the downward pointing arrow with a line above it located at the end of the line of symbols.

Click on any command you want that isn't currently visible to select it or click on one you no longer want to unselect it. The checkmarks next to each item indicate which are visible. For example, here the Save command is checked but none of the others are.

The Quick Access Toolbar can be useful if there's something you're doing repeatedly that's located on a different tab than something else you're doing repeatedly.

Control Shortcut

Throughout this document, I'm going to mention various control shortcuts that you can use to perform tasks like save, copy, cut, and paste like I did above with Select All, Ctrl +A.

Each of these will be written as Ctrl + a capital letter.

When you use the shortcut you do not need to use the capitalized version of the letter. For example, holding down the Ctrl key and the s key at the same time will save your document. I'll write this as Ctrl + S, but that just means hold down the key that says ctrl and the s key at the same time.

Undo

One of the most powerful control shortcuts in PowerPoint is the Undo option. If you do something you didn't mean or that you want to take back, use Ctrl + Z. This will reverse whatever you just did.

If you need to reverse more than one item, you can keep using Ctrl + Z until you've undone everything you wanted to undo, or you can use the Undo option in the Quick Access Toolbar.

If you use the Quick Access Toolbar there is a dropdown menu option that lets you choose to undo multiple steps at once.

Either way, though, you have to undo things in order. So if I bold, underline, and italicize text and want to undo the bolding on the text, I would also have to undo the italics and underline since those happened after I bolded the text. I can't choose to just undo the bolding. Undo walks you backwards one thing at a time.

(Which is why in that example, it might be easier to just unbold the text rather than try to use undo.)

Absolute Basics

Now let's discuss some absolute basics, like opening, closing, saving, and deleting presentations.

Start a New PowerPoint Presentation

To start a brand new PowerPoint presentation, I choose PowerPoint from my applications menu or click on the shortcut I have on my computer's taskbar. If you're already in PowerPoint and want to start a new PowerPoint presentation you can go to the File tab and choose New from the left-hand menu.

You can also use Ctrl + N to start a new presentation. That will bring up a Title Slide that has no theme and is just plain white.

Using the File→New option will give you a choice of a number of different presentations that are pre-formatted. The blank presentation option is also available, but I recommend using one of the pre-formatted options when you can since they've already thought through complementary colors and imagery and font choices.

Clicking on any of the themes will bring up a secondary display. You can actually use the arrows on the left- and right-hand sides of that display to navigate through the template choices and see a little description related to each template.

For some of the templates there will be variant versions shown. For example, for me if I click on the Circuit presentation template it shows that there are four color palettes available. I can click on any of the four variants to use that color palette. Here I've clicked on the gray option instead of the blue:

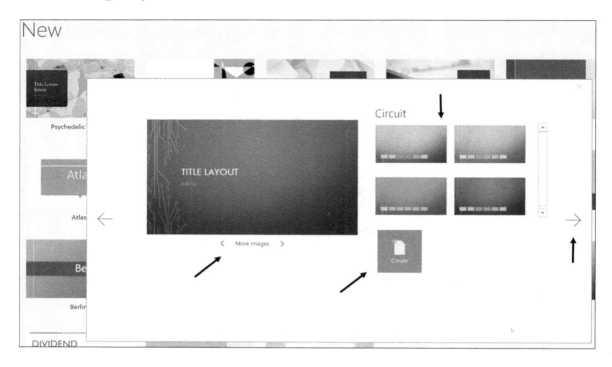

Also, some of the templates may have a More Images option underneath the title slide image. You can click on the arrows there to see what the interior slide layouts for that template will look like.

This can be important because, for example, if you're going to print a presentation chances are you don't want the main presentation slides to use a colored background. You'll want to instead use a template like Ion Boardroom that has a white background on the main presentation slides.

And don't worry if you choose a "bad" template initially. You can change the template and the variant on that template later if you realize the template you chose isn't going to work for you.

Okay, then.

Once you've found a template you like, click on it and then on Create to have PowerPoint start a draft presentation for you to work from.

The presentation should appear with a Title page that has draft text showing on it, usually "Click to Add Title" and often "Click to Add Subtitle."

As I mentioned above, you can always choose a template after you've started working on your presentation using the Design tab which we'll cover later. But if you chose a blank presentation using Ctrl + N you will also have a Design Ideas task pane appear.

I wouldn't recommend using one of the options from the Design Ideas task pane, though, because as far as I can tell it only provides you with a style for the title slide and not the rest of the presentation.

I don't see a way to then have the rest of the slides in your presentation match that title slide style. So the rest of your presentation would still be plain white with black text if you chose one of those options, which isn't very helpful.

Okay, then. That's how to start a brand new presentation. If you have a corporate template you're working from, chances are you'll need to use that instead, so let's talk about how to open an existing presentation next.

Open an Existing PowerPoint File

To open an existing PowerPoint file you can go to the folder where the file is saved and double-click on the file name. Or you can open PowerPoint without selecting a file and it will provide a list of recent documents to choose from under the Recent heading in the middle of the screen.

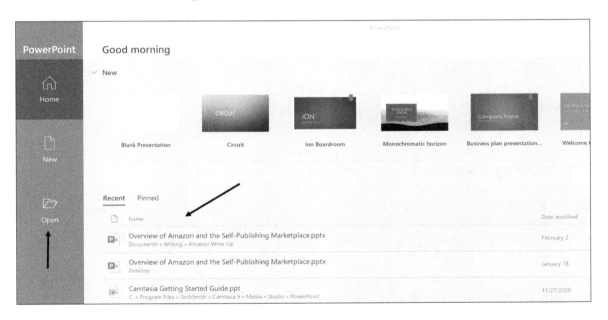

Double-click on one of those file names and the presentation will open.

Next to the Recent heading is a Pinned heading. If you have any presentations that you always want to be able to access easily you can pin them and no matter how long it's been since you opened that presentation last you'll be able to find it under the Pinned heading.

To pin a file, single-click on its name under Recent and look to the right-hand side of the listing. There should be a small thumbtack image. Click on that and the file will be added to the Pinned section.

To unpin a file, just click on the thumbtack again.

If you're in PowerPoint and don't see the file you want under either Recent or Pinned, you can either click on More Presentations at the bottom of the recent files listing or click on the Open option on the left-hand sidebar. Both will bring you to the Open screen.

You can also reach the screen by using Ctrl + O.

The right-hand side of the screen contains your recent presentations once more, but this time you just need to single left-click to open a presentation.

There is also an option there for Folders. This will generally display the folders that those recent presentations are saved in so it's only useful if you know that the presentation you want is stored in the same folder as one you recently used.

Click on the folder name and PowerPoint will display for you all presentations stored in that folder.

What I normally need on this screen is the Browse option that's available to the left of the presentations/folders listing. Left-clicking on that brings up the Open dialogue box which allows you to navigate to any location on your computer. Mine by default opens to the Documents folder.

Once you find the file you want, either click on it and then choose Open, or double-click on it.

Save a PowerPoint File

To quickly save your presentation, you can use Ctrl + S or click on the small image of a floppy disk in the Quick Access Toolbar.

For a document you've already saved that will overwrite the prior version of the document with the current version and will keep the file name, file type, and file location the same.

If you need to change the file name, type, or location you'll need to use the Save As option instead. This can be accessed via the File tab.

(With respect to file type, I sometimes need to, for example, save a presentation as a .pdf or a .jpg file instead.)

When you use Save As you wil need to navigate to where you want to save your file by either clicking on one of the listed file names or by clicking on one of the locations on the left-hand side.

Here I've clicked on Browse which opens a Save As dialogue box that shows the default name PowerPoint assigned, the default file type, and which shows my Documents folder so that I can navigate to where I want to save the file.

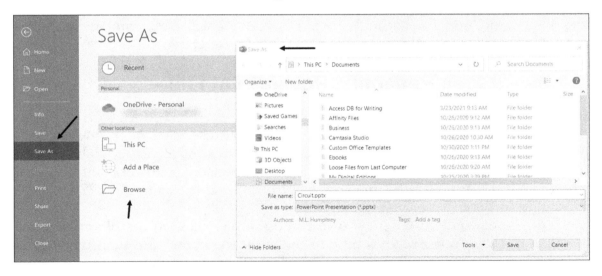

There are still defaults for name and format, but you'll want to change the name of the document to something better than the template name.

If you try to save a file that has never been saved before, it will automatically default to the Save As option and open a dialogue box which requires that you specify where to save the file and what to name it.

Save this file

File Name

Circuit   .pptx

Choose a Location

Documents
Documents

More options...   Save   Cancel

Clicking on More Options will let you also change the file type before you save. It does so by taking you to the Save As screen.

If you had already saved the file and you choose to Save As but keep the same location, name, and format as before, PowerPoint will overwrite the previous version of the file just like it would have if you'd used Save.

Rename a PowerPoint File

If you just want to rename a file, it's best to close the file and then go to where the file is saved and rename it that way rather than use Save As. Using Save As will keep the original of the file as well as creating the newer version. That's great when you want version control (which is rarely needed for PowerPoint), but not when you just wanted to rename your file from Great Presentation v22 to Great Presentation FINAL.

To do so, navigate to where you've saved the file, click on the file name once to select it, click on it a second time to highlight the name, and then type in the new name you want to use, replacing the old one. If you rename the file this way outside of PowerPoint, there will only be one version of the file left, the one with the new name you wanted.

Just be aware that if you rename a file by navigating to where it's located and changing the name you won't be able to access the file from the Recent Presentations list under Open since that will still list the old name which no longer exists. The next time you want to open that file you'll need to navigate to where it's stored and open it that way.

Delete a PowerPoint File

You can't delete a PowerPoint file from within PowerPoint. You need to close the file you want to delete and then navigate to where the file is stored and delete the file from there without opening it.

To do so, locate the file and click on the file name. (Only enough to select it. Make sure you haven't double-clicked and highlighted the name which will delete the file name but not the file.) Next, choose Delete from the menu at the top of the screen, or right-click and choose Delete from the dropdown menu.

Close a PowerPoint File

To close a PowerPoint file click on the X in the top right corner or go to File and then choose Close. (You can also use Ctrl + W, but I never have.)

If no changes have been made to the document since you saved it last, it will just close.

If changes have been made, PowerPoint should ask you if you want to save those changes. You can either choose to save them, not save them, or cancel closing the document and leave it open. I almost always default to saving any changes. If I'm in doubt about whether I'd be overwriting something important, I cancel and choose to Save As and save the current file as a later version of the document just in case (e.g., Great Presentation v2).

If you had copied an image or a large block of text before trying to close your presentation, you may also have a dialogue box pop up asking if you want to keep that image or text available for use when you close the document. Usually the answer to this is no, but if you had planned on pasting that image or text somewhere else and hadn't yet done so, you can say to keep it on the clipboard.

* * *

Okay. Now let's talk about your workspace. We touched on it a bit when we defined task panes, but I want to go over it in more detail now.

Your Workspace

Whether you choose to start a brand new file or open an existing file, you'll end up in the main workspace for PowerPoint. It looks something like this:

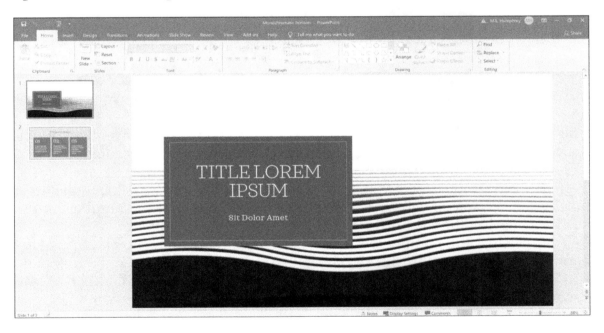

We'll walk through this in more detail in the Working with Your Presentation Slides section but I just wanted you to see right now that there's a left-hand task pane that shows all of the slides in the presentation and then a main section of the screen that shows the slide you're currently working on.

For a new presentation there's usually just the one title slide. This one happens to have two slides that it opens with.

The business presentation template opens with fourteen slides. Let's look through that one now:

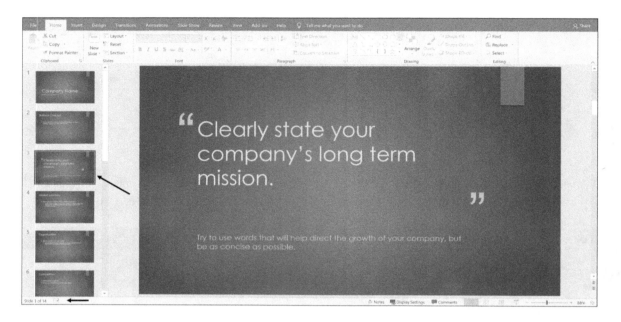

The main portion of the screen will contain the slide you're currently working on. So in this case I've selected a slide from farther into the presentation that is a Quote Name Card slide.

In the left-hand task pane the thumbnail of the slide that is visible in the main portion of the screen will have a dark border around it and the number on the left-hand side of the slide will also be colored a different color.

Your slides will be numbered starting at 1. The number is shown on the left-hand side of the thumbnail for each slide in the task pane. Below the task pane you can see how many slides are in the presentation and the number of the current slide. So here that says 3 of 14.

Both the task pane and the main workspace have scroll bars that let you navigate through the presentation. To move to a different slide you can also double-click on its thumbnail in the task pane and it will appear in the main workspace.

In the bottom right corner you can also change the zoom level for the main workspace. (I usually leave that alone, though.)

Across the top of the workspace are your menu tabs which you may need to use when formatting the text or appearance of your presentation.

There are also dropdown menus available in both the task pane and the main workspace. In the task pane dropdown you have the options to cut, copy, paste, add a new slide, duplicate a slide, delete a slide, add a section (which is an intermediate-level topic), change the slide layout, and more. These relate to the slides themselves.

In the main workspace you also have a dropdown with cut, copy, and paste options, but these generally relate to the text on a slide. There are also options for font, paragraph, bullets, numbering, and more.

We'll revisit some of this later, but for now let's focus on that left-hand task pane and what you can do there with respect to your slides.

Edit Presentation Slides

Before we continue I want to edit your presentation slides, most of which is done by working in the left-hand slide task pane.

Add a Slide

If you right-click into the blank space below your slide(s) in the left-hand task pane, you'll see a dropdown menu that includes the New Slide option.

Click on that and PowerPoint will add a new slide to your presentation. The layout of the slide will either match the layout of the slide directly above it or will be a Title and Content slide if the slide directly above it was a Title slide.

You can also right-click on an existing slide and choose New Slide from that dropdown menu as well. If you do that, the slide that is added to your presentation will have the same layout as the one you right-clicked on.

Another option is to go to the Slides section of the Home tab and click on New Slide there. If you add a slide via the Home tab and click on the New Slide dropdown arrow you can choose the layout you want. (See the chapter on slide layouts for a discussion of the various layout options.)

Select a Slide or Slides

To select a single slide, you simply left-click on the slide where it's visible in the left-hand slide task pane. When a slide is selected it should have a darker border around it. In my version that border appears to be a dark red.

If you want to select more than one slide, left-click on the first slide and then hold down the Ctrl key as you left-click on the other slides you want.

Each selected slide will have that dark border around it.

Slides do not need to be next to one another for you to select them this way.

If you have a range of slides that you want to select, you can use the Shift key instead. Click on the slide at the top or the bottom of the range of slides you want, hold down the Shift key, and then click on the slide at the other end of the range of slides you want. All slides within that range, including both of the slides you clicked, will be selected.

(You can also combine methods of selecting slides to, for example, select a range of slides using Shift and then select an additional slide using the Ctrl key.)

No matter how many slides you select, the main workspace will only show one of them.

To remove your selection of multiple slides, click in the gray area around any of the slides or into your main workspace.

Move a Slide or Slides

The easiest way to move a slide or slides to a different position within your presentation is to select the slide(s) (as noted above) and then left-click and drag the slide(s) to the new location using the left-hand slide task pane.

As you move your chosen slide(s) you'll see the slides moving upward or downward to leave a space for your slide(s) to be inserted.

If you're moving more than one slide, you can left-click on any of the slides you've selected and drag.

All of the selected slides will move to the new location even if they weren't next to one another before.

As you move multiple slides at once you'll see a number in the top right corner telling you how many slides you're moving.

Cut a Slide or Slides

Cutting a slide removes it from its current location but lets you paste that slide elsewhere.

In the task pane, you can right-click on your chosen slide(s) and choose Cut from the dropdown menu. Or you can select your slide(s) and then use Ctrl + X. Or you can select your slide(s) and then go to the Clipboard section of the Home tab and choose Cut from there.

Any of these options will remove the slide(s) from their current position but let you paste them either into another location in that presentation or into another presentation altogether. (Usually within the same presentation I'd just move the slides, but if it was a very long presentation it might be easier to cut and paste instead.)

Copy a Slide or Slides

Copying a slide keeps that slide in its current position but takes a copy of the slide that you can then paste elsewhere.

In the left-hand task pane, you can right-click on your chosen slide(s) and choose Copy from the dropdown menu. Or you can select your slide(s) and then use Ctrl + C. Or you can select your slide(s) in the task pane and then go to the Clipboard section of the Home tab and choose Copy from there.

You also have a Duplicate option in PowerPoint which will take a copy of your selected slide(s) and immediately paste that copy below the selected slide(s). It's available if you right-click or if you click on the dropdown arrow next to Copy in the Clipboard section of the Home tab.

This means you only need to use Copy if you want to paste your copied slide(s) elsewhere in your document or into another presentation.

Paste a Slide or Slides

If you copy or cut a slide or slides and want to use them elsewhere, you need to paste them into that new location.

You can do a basic paste by clicking into the space where you want to put those slides (so between two existing slides or in the gray space at the end of the presentation, for example) and using Ctrl + V.

If you are clicked onto a slide when you use Ctrl + V, your copied or cut slides will be pasted in below that slide you were clicked onto.

You can also right-click where you want to paste a slide and choose from the paste options in the dropdown menu.

The first option, which has a small a in the bottom right corner, is Use Destination Theme. If you're cutting or copying and pasting within an existing presentation this won't mean much. I have used this one, however, when working with a corporate PowerPoint template where someone had drafted their presentation slides without using the template and I had to bring their content into the corporate template.

In a situation like that you can copy all of the slides from the initial version of the presentation and paste them into the corporate template using the destination theme option which will convert the slides from whatever theme was initially used to the corporate theme. You'll still have to walk through your document and make sure nothing was impacted by the change of theme, but at least you won't have to change each slide's theme individually.

The second paste option you have, the one with the paintbrush in the bottom right corner, is Keep Source Formatting. This does exactly what it says, it keeps the formatting that the slide(s) already had.

Sometimes it's important to do this especially if you've done a lot of custom work on a slide and don't want your images, charts, etc. resized when you move them into a new presentation.

The third paste option, the one with a photo icon in the bottom right corner, is to paste a slide in as a Picture. That means the slide can no longer be edited. It's like someone took a snapshot of that slide and now you just have that snapshot. If you try to use this option with multiple slides only the first slide will paste in.

You can also paste slides by going to the Clipboard section of the Home tab and choosing Paste from there. The more advanced paste options are available by clicking on the arrow under Paste.

Delete a Slide

To delete a slide, you can click on that slide in the left-hand task pane and then hit the Delete or Backspace key. Either one will work. Or you can right-click on that slide and choose Delete Slide from the dropdown menu.

Reset a Slide

If you make changes to the layout of a slide, by for example changing the size of the text boxes or their location, and want to go back to the original layout for that slide type for that theme, you can right-click on the slide and choose Reset Slide from the dropdown menu. According to PowerPoint, this will "reset the position, size, and formatting of the slide placeholders to their default settings."

You can also do so by clicking on the slide you want to reset and clicking on the Reset option in the Slides section of the Home tab.

Presentation Themes

As a beginner, I highly recommend that you work with the presentation themes that PowerPoint provides you rather than trying to create a presentation from scratch. Presentation themes are pre-built to use colors, fonts, and imagery that all work together to provide a polished appearance.

As a matter of fact, the rest of this guide will assume that that's what you're doing. I do not cover here how to create a presentation from scratch.

We already covered above under how to create a new presentation how to start your presentation using one of the PowerPoint themes or a variation on that theme. This chapter will cover how to change your presentation theme once you've started to create your presentation.

There are a number of reasons why you might want to do so. For example, the audiences I've presented to in the past expect the title field on each slide to appear at the top of the slide. There are a handful of PowerPoint themes that place the title portion of the slide elsewhere. So if I were to inadvertently select one of those as I started to prepare, I'd need to change it once I realized that.

Also, some of the themes include a wider variety of slide layouts than others. If I knew I'd be using a certain slide layout that wasn't available in my chosen theme it might be easier to switch to a theme that did have that slide layout rather than try to create it myself.

So. How do you do this? How do you change your theme once you've started working on a presentation?

First, go to the Design tab.

You should see that the Themes section takes up most of the tab starting on the left-hand side of the screen. The first thumbnail in that section is your current theme followed by your other choices.

To see how each theme will look, you can hold your mouse over the thumbnail for that theme and PowerPoint will temporarily apply it to the slide in your main workspace.

To see more themes, click on the down arrow at the end. To see all themes at once, click on the down arrow with a line above it. That will give you something that looks like this:

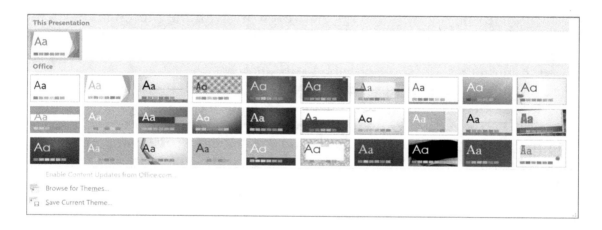

I recommend when choosing a theme that you look at how that theme will appear when applied to both a Title slide as well as a Title and Content slide before making your choice, because they can be very different.

For example, the slide on the next page is from the Integral theme and is very simple. But the title slide for that theme is dominated by a decorative pattern that is not.

Also, theoretically, the text color that will be used in the headers on your presentation is the same one used for the Aa on the thumbnail image but it's good to confirm that by seeing the theme on a slide.

And the colored boxes that run along the bottom of each thumbnail do show the main color palette for the theme, but most themes will only use the first color or two for bullets or effects.

For example, here is a slide using the Integral theme and it only uses one accent color:

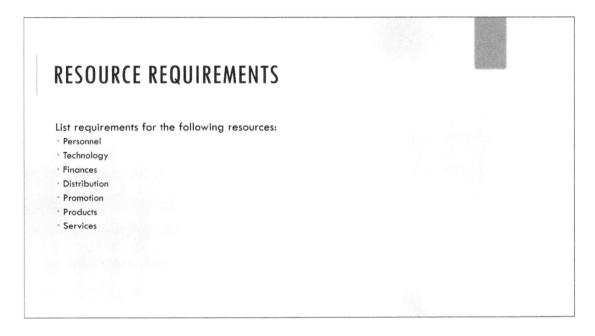

If you add charts, etc. you will see more of the theme colors used and they are all available for any text, element, etc. color choice that you make.

So always a good idea to preview your themes. And to do so on both a title slide and a content slide. (If you don't already have a content slide, right-click in the left-hand task pane and choose New Slide.)

Once you've found a theme you like, to permanently apply it to your slides, simply click on it.

That should apply the theme to every slide in your entire presentation. But it won't do so if you'd selected a subset of your slides before choosing the theme. It also may not do so if your presentation has sections in it.

(Which is why it's always good to start with the right theme so that you don't have to worry about these issues later.)

In addition to the choices you can see in the Themes section of the Design tab, some themes also have what are called variants. Variants use the same structure and design elements but have different color palettes or use different background colors or patterns.

Not every theme has a variant, but when a theme does have variants you will see them in the Variants section of the Design tab.

They only appear after you have selected that specific theme. Here, for example, is the variant section for the Integral theme.

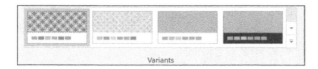

Variants

The first thumbnail is the default option for that theme. The remaining thumbnails show the variants.

Just like with the Themes section if there are more than three variants available you can use the arrows on the right-hand side to see the rest of the choices.

Also, as with the theme thumbnails, you can hold your mouse over each variant to see what it will look like when applied to your presentation.

In this example, at least two of the variants use a non-white background for the main slides in the presentation. A couple also use more than one of the theme colors, so there can definitely be some variety within a theme.

But they all do keep the general design elements the same. Here is an example of one of the variants for the Integral theme:

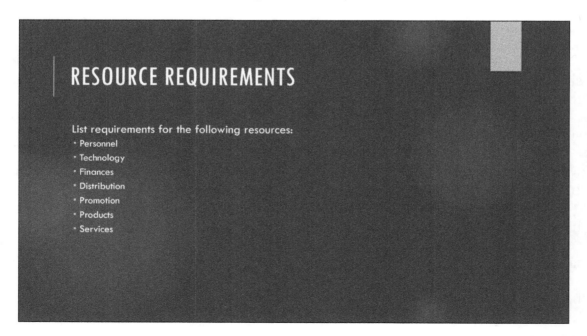

Be careful when applying a new theme that all of your existing slides work with that new theme. It is possible for the main slides to work but the title slide to no longer have an acceptable appearance. Or vice versa.

If you find a presentation theme that you like but still can't find colors that work for you amongst the variant thumbnails, you can instead change the colors using the Colors dropdown menu under Variants in the Design tab.

To access it, click on the downward arrow with a line on the right-hand side of the Variants thumbnail display. That will bring up a dropdown menu that includes the Colors option. Hold your mouse over that Colors option and a secondary dropdown menu will appear that shows various color palettes.

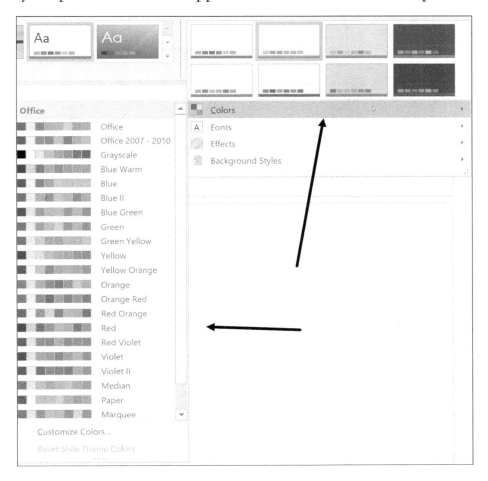

Just like with the theme and variant thumbnails, you can hold your mouse over each color palette to see how it will appear in your presentation. Click on one to permanently apply it.

Changing your theme should definitely not be the last thing you do. Ideally you choose a theme before you start to add your content so that you can adjust as you add your content. But in case it's needed, that's how you do it.

Okay, then. Now let's talk about the various slide layouts that may be available as part of each theme.

Slide Layouts

There are a variety of slide layouts available to you in PowerPoint. Probably more than you'll actually need. But I wanted to run through a handful of the most common ones before we go any farther because I'm going to occasionally refer to a slide layout and I want you to know what I'm talking about when I do.

The images below use the Facet theme with a customized color palette applied.

As mentioned above, to add a new slide into your presentation, right-click in the left-hand task pane and choose New Slide from the dropdown menu.

Or you can go to the Insert tab and choose New Slide from the Slides section. If you click on the dropdown arrow, you can then choose your layout before you insert the slide.

To change the layout of a slide you've already added to your presentation, right-click on the slide, go to Layout, and choose a new layout from the secondary dropdown menu.

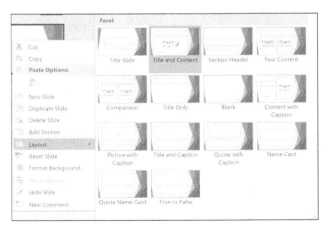

You can also select a slide or slides, go to the Slides section of the Home tab, click on the dropdown arrow next to Layout, and choose your layout from there.

Not all themes or templates will have all layouts. And different themes may have the elements (such as text boxes) of a layout in different locations on the slide. For example, the Slice theme puts the title section of each slide at the bottom of the page instead of the top.

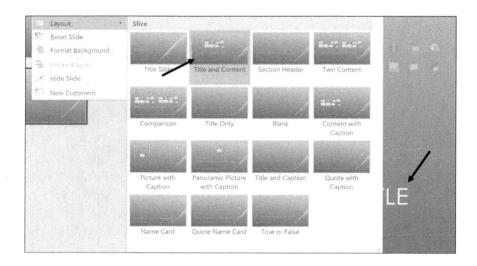

This is why you should definitely look at where the elements are in a presentation theme before you decide to use it.

* * *

Now let's walk through your slide layout choices. In my opinion, you can put together a perfectly adequate presentation with just the Title and Title and Content slides, although there are many more choices than that.

Title Slide

The Title slide is the default first slide for a presentation. It has a section for adding a title and a subtitle and, if you choose one of the templates provided in PowerPoint, a background or design elements that match the chosen theme.

Section Header

If you are going to have sections within your presentation, then you'll want to separate them using a Section Header slide.

This slide has an appearance that is close to that of the title slide, but usually the text or design elements are in a different position. It may also use different colors, fonts, or font colors.

In this theme you can see that the design element on the left-hand side is slightly different from the one used for the title slide. The text is also located in a different location and is a smaller font size.

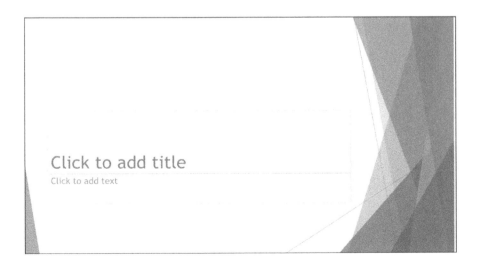

Title and Content Slide

The Title and Content slide is the one I use for most of my presentations. For a basic presentation with a bulleted set of talking points, this is the slide that you'll probably use the most often.

It has a text box where you can give a high-level title for the slide and then a larger text box that takes up most of the rest of the space on the slide where you can add text or a data table, chart, picture, video, etc.

The design elements on this slide are generally less pronounced than on the title and section slides, but not always.

Here you can see that the design elements are the same as were used on the section slide but that the amount of space for text is much larger and the title is at the top.

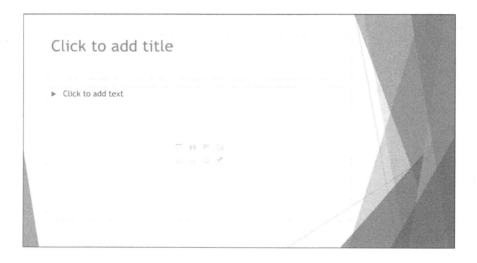

Be careful when moving between themes to check your titles on your slides. Some themes use all caps in the title section and some do not. If you're switching between a theme that uses all caps to one that doesn't, you may find that you need to retype your entries because only half of your words are capitalized the way they should be.

Two Content

The Two Content slide is another content slide. This slide has a section for a title and then two separate content boxes. It can be a good choice for when you want to either have two separate bulleted lists side by side or when you want to have text next to an image, data table, video, or chart.

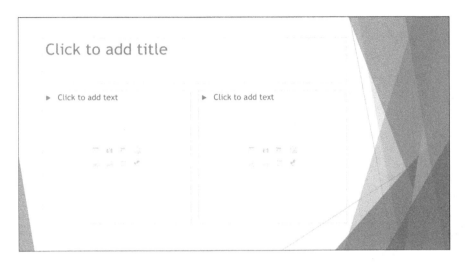

* * *

It can be hard to see the difference between the different slide types when they don't have content in them, so here's a snapshot from the left-hand task pane of the first four slide types we've discussed with content added to them using the Facet theme and then using the Ion Boardroom theme.

The content is exactly the same for both:

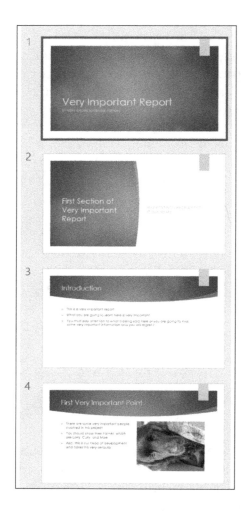

Note that when I changed the theme over to Ion Boardroom it changed the orientation of the image I'd placed on the fourth slide. If you move between themes you need to always go back through your presentation and make sure that all of your text, bullet points, images, etc. still work with the new theme.

* * *

Okay, then. Next slide type.

Comparison

The Comparison slide is a content slide much like the Two Content slide except it has added sections directly above each of the two main text boxes where you can put header text to describe the contents of each of the boxes.

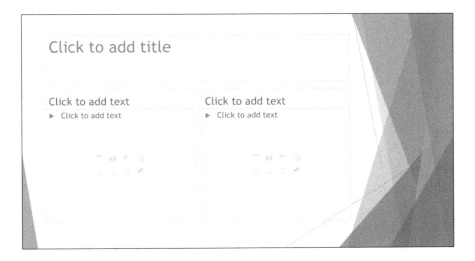

This is especially good for situations where you maybe have side-by-side charts, data tables, videos, or images and you want to be able to label each one.

Title Only

The Title Only slide is a content slide that just has the title section and nothing else. You would generally use this slide when you wanted to add elements to the body of the slide yourself or when you wanted to separate sections and didn't want to use the section header slide.

Blank

The Blank slide has the design elements common to all of the content slides but there are no text boxes on the slide at all.

Content With Caption

The Content With Caption slide is a content slide where the title section covers half of the screen and there are two text boxes where you can add text, images, etc. One of the text boxes is below the title and the other takes up the other half of the slide.

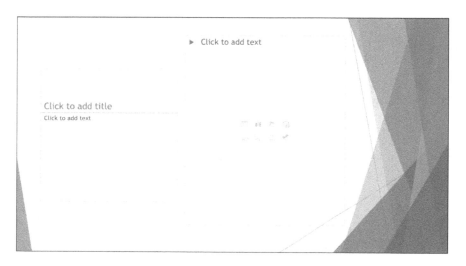

Picture With Caption

The Picture With Caption slide has a large section for a picture and then a text box below it where you can add a title and description of the picture.

Title And Caption

The Title And Caption slide has a large section for a title with a smaller section for text. It would make a good section separator if you wanted a different appearance for a new section such as an Appendix.

Quote With Caption

The Quote With Caption slide is a slide that has quote marks around the main text section and then a smaller text box immediately under that for an attribution of who said the quote. There's also another text box for comments related to the quote.

Other

Some themes will have even more pre-formatted slide types you can use. For example, the Ion Boardroom theme has a three-column slide type and this theme had a Name Card option.

Some themes won't have this many. In that case you can either create what you need by adding on to the Blank or Title Only slides or you can find a theme that better suits your needs.

As I said before, I can put together a perfectly good presentation using the Title and Title and Content slides alone, but it is nice to have more options than that to work with. A presentation where every single slide looks the same can become monotonous and that can lose you the attention of your audience. Although, as always, you need to balance that out against making your presentation more interesting than what you're saying.

Alright, now let's cover how to add content to a slide.

Add and Format Text

Add Text

Adding text to an existing slide is very easy. You simply click and type. For example, here, is a Title slide:

See where it says "Click to add title" and "Click to add subtitle"? Those are both text boxes that are already set up for you to add your text. All you have to do is click on either one and start typing.

When you're done typing in one text box you can click in the other or click elsewhere on the slide.

It works the same for content-style slides. The main Title and Content slide has a text box where it says "Click to add title" and a text box where it says "Click to add text". With this particular theme, the main text is shown as a bulleted list, so you'll see the first bullet is already there and a new bullet will appear each time you hit Enter..

Here is one of those slides completed with three rows of talking points:

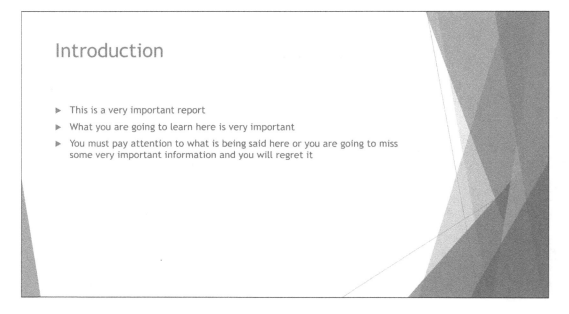

All I had to do was click into the text box and start typing. Each time I hit Enter it started a new line for me that already had a bullet point.

If you need to create subpoints you can use the tab key to indent a line before you start typing your text.

In some templates that will also change the type of bullet used or change the size of the bullet. It will often also change the size of the text. In this next image you can clearly see that the third-level of text is smaller than the first level. In fact, each line goes down by 2 pts in this theme. So the first line is 18 pt, the next is 16 pt, and the third is 14 pt.

To remove an indent, use Shift + Tab before your start typing.

For lines that have already been added where you need to adjust the indent, click to the left of the first letter in that line and then use Tab or Shift + Tab to adjust the indent.

You can also use the Decrease List Level and Increase List Level options in the Paragraph section of the Home tab. They're the ones with lines with an arrow pointing either left or right in the middle of the top row of that section. You can click anywhere on that paragraph to use the option; you don't have to click at the start of the text.

If you want complete control over your indent, you can right-click and choose Paragraph from the dropdown menu. This will bring up the Paragraph dialogue box where you can specify an exact indent amount.

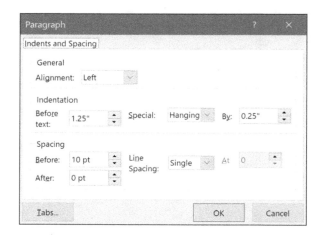

By default the PowerPoint themes use fonts and font sizes that are legible for a presentation given on a projector. That's true for probably the first three levels of indents. But past that point the text may become too small to be legible from a distance.

I wouldn't go below about 14 point for any text on a slide that's meant to be used in a presentation. (As opposed to printed out.) I believe that most of the pre-formatted presentations stop decreasing the font size at 12 point, which may be workable but is just on the edge for me.

Also, sometimes PowerPoint will adjust your text dynamically to make it fit into the text box. So if you use too much text it will make that text smaller than the default in order to get the text to fit.

Because this can happen on a slide-by-slide basis it creates a disjointed presentation when it happens. If one slide has bullet points in a 20 point size and another has bullet points in a 14 point size and another has them in an 11 point size, even if the font and colors are consistent across slides, it can be distracting to a viewer.

Which is why I try when I can to make the font size consistent across slides. The easiest way to do so is to keep your entries short and sweet.

In other words, don't have one slide with a title of "Introduction" and another with a title of "Discussion of the Philosophical Aspects of Polar Ionization and Government Regulatory Structures". Chances are that second slide will automatically be converted to a smaller font size (and may have text that runs outside of the provided text box to boot.)

With bullet points try to keep it to three levels or less. If you can't do that, consider manually adjusting the font size for the fourth-level and beyond bullet points.

And if you absolutely can't avoid lengthy text, then adjust the rest of your slides to the size of the lengthiest text entries. For example, with the Facet theme I've been using here, the default title size is 36 point, but when I put in a very lengthy title it is reduced to 32 point. So to create consistency throughout the presentation I'd change any 36 point titles to 32 point.

(Obviously, it's easier to simplify the language instead, but that's not always an option when working on group projects or with a boss who has certain unmovable notions of what should be said.)

Move Text

If you need to cut, copy, or paste text from within a slide, it works much the same way as it did for the slides in the left-hand pane.

To cut text, highlight the text you want to cut and then use Ctrl + X or go to the Clipboard section of the Home tab and choose Cut from there. You can also right-click and choose Cut from the dropdown menu.

As you'll recall, cutting text removes it from its current location but still allows you to paste that text elsewhere.

To copy text, highlight the text you want to copy and then use Ctrl + C or to go to the Clipboard section of the Home tab and choose Copy from there. You can also right-click and choose Copy from the dropdown menu.

Copying keeps the text in its current location but also allows you to paste that text elsewhere.

To paste text, click on the location where you want to place the text you copied or cut and then use Ctrl + V. If you paste text this way it will take on the formatting of the location where you paste it.

Your other options are to click where you want to paste the text and then either go to the Clipboard section of the Home tab and click on the arrow under Paste or right-click and choose one of the paste options from the dropdown menu.

The paste option with the lower case a in the bottom right corner (Use Destination Theme) will use the formatting of the location where you are pasting your text. So font, etc., but it might still keep the font size.

The option with the paintbrush in the bottom right corner (Keep Source Formatting) will keep the formatting the text already had.

The option with the small picture in the bottom right corner (Picture) will paste the selected text in as an image. (You will not be able to edit this text after it's pasted because it will no longer be considered text.)

The option with the large A in the bottom right corner (Keep Text Only), will paste the text into the presentation but use the formatting that would apply to any text you typed into that specific location.

Here I have taken the word Introduction from the title section of a slide and I have pasted it into four separate bullet points that were formatted to use 12 pt Algerian for the font. (So basically a different font, different font size, and different color.)

You can see that for Use Destination Theme (1) it changed the font size and color but not the font. For Keep Source Formatting (2) nothing changed. For Picture (3) it inserted the text exactly as it existed originally but as a picture. And for Keep Text Only (4) the font, font size, and font color all changed.

Ctrl + V gives the same result as the first line (1), so change of color and size but not font.

Basically, if you're moving text around you may need to do some formatting once it moves unless you remember to Paste – Keep Text Only.

Alright. That's copy/cut and paste. There are more specialized paste options available under the Clipboard option, but for a beginner level I don't think they're worth discussing here. If you want to look at them click on Paste Special from the dropdown to bring up the Paste Special dialogue box.

Delete Text

If you need to remove text you can either cut that text or you can use the Delete or Backspace keys. Backspace will delete text to the left of the cursor. Delete will delete text to the right of the cursor.

If you've highlighted the text you want to delete then either one will work.

Delete and Backspace can also delete bullet points or the numbers or letters in a numbered list.

Change Font Size

To adjust font size, you have a few options.

First, whichever option you use will require you to make the change before you start typing or to highlight any text you have already typed that you want to change. So do that.

Next, your first option is to go to the Font section of the Home tab and use the font size dropdown to choose a new font size. The current font size should appear in that box unless you've selected text that is more than one size. If that happens, the value will show the smallest font size with a plus sign next to it. So for me just now when I selected four levels of bullet points it showed as 12+ but when I then only selected the top two levels it showed as 16+.

You can either click on the dropdown arrow and select one of the listed font sizes or you can type in your own value.

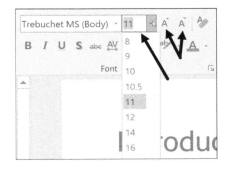

Another way to change the font size is located to the right of the dropdown. There are two capital A's with an arrow in the top right corner. One is to increase font size and the other is to decrease font size. Using those options will increase the font size or decrease it by one spot on the dropdown menu.

So if you have a 10 point font and use the increase font size option it will go up to 10.5 because that's the next available font size in the dropdown. But if you're at 14 it will take you to 16 and 36 will go to 40.

Another option you have is to right-click in the main workspace and use what I refer to as the mini formatting menu. It appears either directly above or directly below the dropdown menu and is a miniature version of the Font section of the Home tab. It has both the font size dropdown menu as well as the increase and decrease font options.

Finally, you can right-click in the main workspace and choose Font from the dropdown menu. This will bring up the Font dialogue box which has a Size option. You can either type in the value you want or use the up and down arrows to change the font size. The size will change by .1 with each use of the up or down arrows. So 14 will go to 14.1, for example.

Which means it'll generally be easier to just type in the value you want.

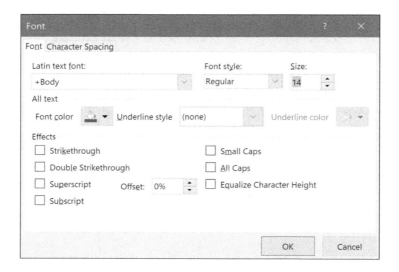

Change Font

In general I wouldn't recommend changing the font because the templates are built to work well with their assigned fonts. But it does sometimes need to be done. For example, a number of my corporate consulting clients have had fonts that they wanted used for all communications to create consistent branding.

As before, you either need to change the font choice before you start typing or you need to select the text you want to change.

Once you've done that, you have a few options for changing your font.

The first is in the Font section of the Home tab. There is a font dropdown menu which is to the left of the font size dropdown menu. In this example the font that's currently in use is Trebuchet MS. To change that font, click on the arrow for the dropdown menu and then click on the font you'd like to use.

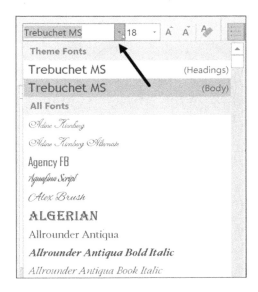

The name of each font in the dropdown menu is written in that font which should help give you an idea of which font to use. I would caution you against using a script (like Aquafina) or a stylized font (like Algerian) for the main text in a presentation slide. A presentation should be about conveying information and the text you use to do that shouldn't get in the way of your communication. Using an overly-ornate font distracts from the text and also from the speaker because your audience is too busy trying to read your slides instead of listen to you.

If you already know the font you want, you can click into the field that shows the current font and start typing the name of the font you'd like. As you type, PowerPoint will auto-complete the field. If you click on the dropdown arrow first and then click into that field and start typing the dropdown list of fonts will move to that part of the alphabet, which comes in handy when the font you want is later in the alphabet.

The mini formatting menu is another available option and works the same way as the Font section of the Home tab.

Or you can right-click and choose Font from the dropdown menu and then change the font choice in the Latin Text Font dropdown menu.

Change Font Color

Another adjustment you might need to make to your text is to change the color of the text. For example, when we discussed the Paste options above some of the options kept the original text color when what would've looked best is changing the font color to black to match the rest of the text in the main body of the slide.

As with all other font choices you either need to make this change before you start typing or you need to select the text you want to change.

Once you've done so click on the arrow next to the A that by default has a red underline in either the Font section of the Home tab or the mini formatting bar.

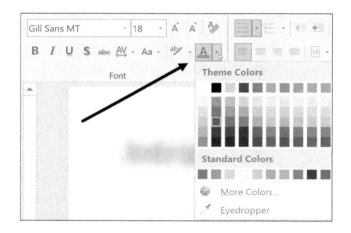

(That line may not always be red. It changes as you change your font color. So the first time you use it, the underline color will change to whatever the last color you used was. This can be useful because then you can just click on the A and apply that color again instead of having to use the dropdown menu each time.)

That initial dropdown menu allows you to choose from one of seventy available colors. Just click on the square for the color you want to use. If you're not sure how a color will look in your presentation, you can hold your mouse over it and your selected text will change to show the color. To apply it, though, you need to click on it.

The Theme Colors section will actually change what colors are shown to you based upon which theme and theme color palette you've chosen. Remember those six colors I mentioned at the bottom of each theme that don't seem to actually get used much? This is where you can find them and apply them yourself as well as shades of each color.

The Standard Colors will not change, however. And if you need a different or a custom color, you can click on the More Colors option which brings up the Colors dialogue box. Within that dialogue box, on the Standard tab you can choose from the honeycomb of colors available by clicking on any of the colored tiles. Or on the Custom tab you can input your own RGB or HSL values.

You can also click into the rainbow of colors above that to select a color or move the black and white slider for different shades of the current color.

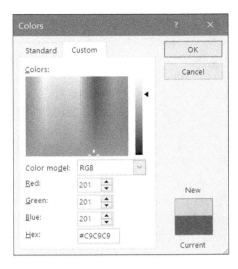

For either the Custom or Standard tab, the color you've selected will show under New in the bottom right corner of the Colors dialogue box and the color you were using previously will show under Current so you can compare them.

When I have corporate clients who have a specified color palette being able to apply the exact right shade of a color using the RGB values is incredibly helpful.

Another option available to you in PowerPoint is the eyedropper. This is for when you already have that color somewhere in your presentation and need to grab it for use elsewhere. For example, I've brought in a cover from a book into a PowerPoint slide so that I could grab the color I need from that cover so that my presentation is consistent with the book it's about.

To use the eyedropper click on the dropdown arrow for Font Color and then choose Eyedropper from the bottom of the dropdown menu. Next, click on the color you want to use from within your presentation. This will change any selected text to that color and will also add the color as a choice under Recent Colors in the Font Color dropdown menu.

Another option for changing your font color is to right-click on your presentation slide and choose Font from the dropdown menu to open the Font dialogue box. On the Font tab you can then click on the dropdown arrow for the Font Color option. It's identical to the other two choices except that it won't have the eyedropper option.

Bold Text

To bold text either select the text you want to bold or make your choice before you start typing.

The easiest option is to use Ctrl + B.

You can also click on the capital B in the bottom row of the Font section of the Home tab or the mini formatting menu.

Or you can right-click, choose Font from the dropdown menu, and then change the Font Style in the Font dialogue box to Bold. Use Bold Italic if you want both bold and italic.

To remove bolding from text, select the text and either click on the capital B or use Ctrl + B once more. If you select text that is partially bolded and partially not bolded, you may need to do this twice because the first time may apply bolding to the entire selection. If that happens then the second time will remove it from the entire selection.

You can also change the Font Style back to Regular in the Font dialogue box.

Italicize Text

To italicize text either select the text you want to italicize or make your choice before you start typing.

The easiest option is to use Ctrl + I.

You can also click on the slanted capital I in the bottom row of the Font section of the Home tab or the mini formatting menu.

Or you can right-click, choose Font from the dropdown menu, and then change the Font Style in the Font dialogue box to Italic. As above, use Bold Italic if you want both bold and italic.

To remove italics from text, select the text and either click on the slanted capital I or use Ctrl + I once more. If you select text that is partially italicized and partially not, you may need to do this twice.

You can also change the Font Style back to Regular in the Font dialogue box.

Underline Text

To underline text either select the text you want to underline or make your choice before you start typing.

The easiest option is to use Ctrl + U. This will place a single underline under your text.

You can also click on the underlined U in the bottom row of the Font section of the Home tab or the mini formatting menu.

If you want a wider variety of choices for how to underline your text, right-click and choose Font from the dropdown menu. You can then click on the arrow for the Underline Style dropdown and choose from a variety of underline styles including a double underline, a darker underline, as well as dashed, dotted, and wavy lines.

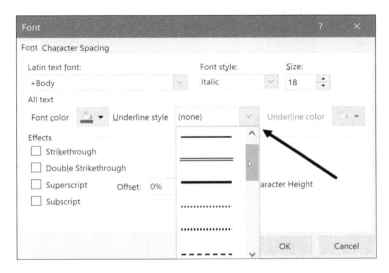

To remove underlining from text, select the text and either click on the capital U with a line under it or use Ctrl + U once more. If you select text that is partially underlined and partially not, you may need to do this twice. If the type of underline was a specialized underline and not the basic single-line style, you will also need to do this twice because the first time you use Ctrl + U or click on the U in the Font section it will convert the specialized underline to a standard single-line underline.

You can also go to the Font dialogue box and change the Underline Style to none, which is the first option.

Change Case

If you want your text to be in all caps or if you have text that is already in all caps that you want to change to normal case, then you will need to change the case of that text.

For this one you have to type the text first and then select it and make the change.

The change case option shows as a capital A followed by a lower-case a, so Aa, and is located in the bottom row of the Font section of the Home tab. It is not an option in the mini formatting menu.

Click on the dropdown arrow to see your available choices and then click on the one you want.

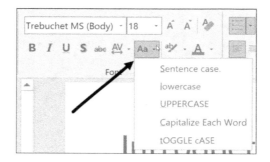

Each choice is written in that style. You can choose between sentence case, lower case, upper case, capitalize each word, and toggle case. (For a presentation unless you have a very good reason for doing so, do not use toggle case.)

Sentence case will capitalize the first letter of the first word in each sentence or text string.

Lower case will put all of the letters in lower case.

Upper case will put all of the letters in upper case.

Capitalize each word will capitalize the first letter of each word.

Toggle case will put the first letter of each word in lower case and all other letters in upper case.

Another option you have is to right-click and choose Font from the dropdown menu but that will only let you apply the upper case option. (By checking the box for all caps).

It does, however, also include an option for small caps which sometimes looks better than using upper case. See here for an example:

```
▶  ALL CAPS
▶  SMALL CAPS
```

Clear Text Formatting

If you've edited a text selection and want to return it to the default for that theme, you can select the text and then click on the small A with an eraser in the top right corner of the Font section. (If you hold your mouse over it, it will show as Clear All Formatting.)

This will change the selection to whatever font, font size, and font formatting would be appropriate for that location within that theme. It does not change the case of the letters if you used the dropdown menu in the Font section, but it will revert the font, font color, font size, and any bold, italics or underline back to the default for the theme.

Other

You'll note that there were a few other options available in the Font section of the Home tab (text shadowing, strikethrough, and character spacing) as well as additional options in the Font dialogue box.

I've chosen not to cover them here because I want to keep this guide focused on a basic level of PowerPoint presentation and those are ones I expect you wouldn't use as often.

But if there's a text effect you want to apply in a PowerPoint slide that I didn't cover, the Font section of the Home tab or right-clicking and choosing Font to bring up the Font dialogue box are generally where you'll find them.

For more advanced text formatting look to the Drawing Tools Format tab which will appear when you click on any text box in your presentation. There you can apply WordArt styles, text fills, text outlines, and text effects.

Okay. Now let's talk about paragraph-level formatting.

Format Paragraphs

What we just talked about are formatting changes that you can make at the level of an individual word. But there are other changes you can make at the paragraph level. These are generally available through the Paragraph section of the Home tab but some of them are also available in the mini formatting menu or by right-clicking and choosing Paragraph from the dropdown menu.

With the paragraph formatting options you don't have to highlight all of the text you want to change, you just need to be clicked somewhere into the paragraph or section you want to change.

Let's start with one we already covered earlier, Decrease List Level and Increase List Level.

Decrease List Level/Increase List Level

A lot of PowerPoint presentations rely on using bulleted lists. And when you use a bulleted list you will often want to either indent the next line or decrease the indent of the next line.

To indent the next line, you can either click at the beginning of the line and use the Tab key, or you can click anywhere on the line and use the Increase List Level option in the Paragraph section of the Home tab. It's the one that has an arrow pointing to the right at a series of lines.

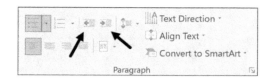

To decrease the indent on a line you can either click at the beginning of the line and use Shift + Tab (so hold down the Shift key and the Tab key at the same time) or you can click anywhere on the line and use the Decease List Level option in the Paragraph section of the Home tab. This is the one with a left-pointing arrow embedded in a series of lines.

If either option is grayed out that's because you can't increase or decrease that indent any further.

These options may or may not be available with plain text that isn't already bulleted or numbered. It will depend on where the text is located within the presentation slide. For example, you generally won't have an indent option in the title section of a slide.

If you have to use very specific placement for your text, you can also right-click and choose Paragraph from the dropdown menu and then use the Paragraph dialogue box to set your indent. It's the value for Before Text in the Indentation section.

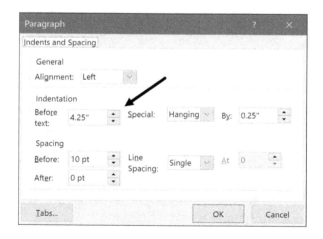

Hanging Indent

Next let's talk about setting a hanging indent or removing one since that's a visible option there in the Paragraph dialogue box and it can be useful to know. (Although keep in mind that if you're working with one of the pre-formatted themes it will likely already have these settings applied and the less you mess with them the better.)

A hanging indent has to do with where your lines of text will start when you have more than one line of text. This is generally used for bulleted and numbered items.

Here is an example where the paragraph is set to have a hanging indent so that the text on all of the lines starts at the same spot. See how the words "also", "development", and "seriously" line up?

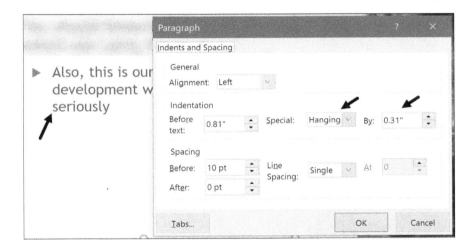

The amount of the indent required to make that happen will be driven by the font and font size. Also by the value you have for "before text".

For each bulleted level on this page the values in the "before text" and "by" fields is different. (This is why it's best not to mess with this and just let PowerPoint do all of it for you.)

If you remove a hanging indent for a bulleted item, it will look like this:

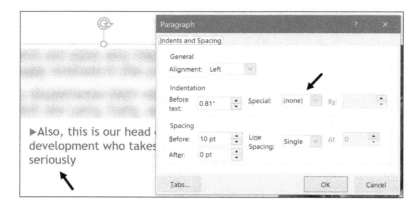

And if you change it to have a first line indent (depending on the value you use), it will look like this:

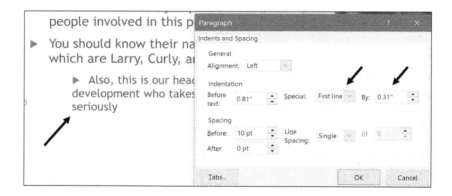

As I said before, I'd generally leave these settings alone, but I have had at least one employer who hadn't created a template for their staff to use, but insisted on very specific indenting for each bulleted item, and the only way to get what they wanted was to adjust these indentation settings.

Okay, then. On to paragraph alignment.

Paragraph Alignment

Your next option is to change the alignment of the text in your paragraph. You have four options.

You can have left-aligned text, meaning that the lines in your paragraph are aligned along the left-hand side.

You can have centered text, meaning each line is aligned along the center.

You can have right-aligned text, meaning each line is aligned along the right-hand side.

Or you can have justified text meaning your text will be spread out across the text box so that it's aligned along both the left- and right-hand side.

Here are examples using the same text where I've copied and pasted it four times and only changed the alignment and the descriptor (left-aligned, centered, etc.)

> ► This is to show you what **left-aligned** text looks like. We need enough text for you to really see how it works.
>
> ► This is to show you what **centered** text looks like. We need enough text for you to really see how it works.
>
> ► This is to show you what **right-aligned** text looks like. We need enough text for you to really see how it works.
>
> ► This is to show you what **justified** text looks like. We need enough text for you to really see how it works.

For bulleted points in the main body of the presentation you can see that left-aligned is generally going to be the choice you want, although justified can work as well. Centered is usually best for headers or titles.

To change the alignment of a paragraph, you can go to the Paragraph section of the Home tab and click on one of the alignment options in the bottom row. Each one is a series of lines that shows its alignment type. Click on the one you want to apply it.

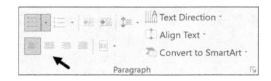

The left, center, and right alignment options are also available in the mini formatting menu.

Or you can right-click, choose Paragraph, and change the alignment using the dropdown menu in the General section. That dropdown has one more option, Distributed which will stretch your line of text across the entire space. I generally don't recommend that for a normal paragraph because the last line won't look good.

Depending on where your text is and what type of text box it is, your selected alignment will either apply to just that paragraph or to all of the contents of the text box. So if you want to use more than one alignment type on a slide (which I generally wouldn't recommend) you may need to use more than one text box to make that happen.

Text Alignment

In addition to setting your paragraph alignment you can also set how the text in a text box will align itself with respect to that text box. Your choices are top, middle, or bottom. Here are examples of each. I've clicked into the middle text box so you can see the outlines of the box. All three paragraphs are in identical text boxes that I've just copied and pasted side-by-side and then changed the alignment to top, middle, and bottom.

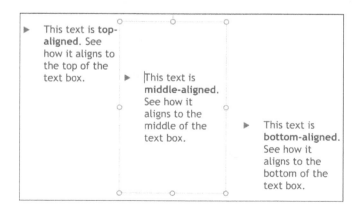

To choose which alignment option you want, go to the Paragraph section of the Home tab and click on the arrow next to Align Text on the right-hand side of the section. This will give you a dropdown menu where you can then click on either Top, Middle, or Bottom.

Your choice will apply to all text within that text box.

If you click on More Options that will open a Format Shape task pane where you can also choose to center the text at the same time.

Using Multiple Columns

If you want your text displayed on a slide in multiple columns you have two choices.

First, you can choose a slide layout that has two equally sized sections like the Two Content slide format and then input your text into both of those boxes, split evenly across the two boxes.

Or, you can use the multiple column formatting option. To split text into multiple columns, simply click anywhere within that text and then go to the Paragraph section of the Home tab and click on the arrow next to the Add or Remove Columns option. (This is the one in the center of the bottom row of that section that shows two sets of lines side by side with a dropdown arrow on the right-hand side.) It is directly to the right of the left, center, right, and justify paragraph options.

You can choose between One Column, Two Columns, Three Columns, or More Columns.

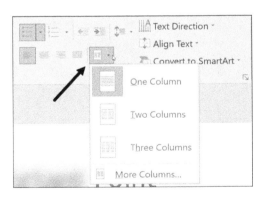

If you click on More Columns you can specify not only the number of columns, but the spacing between them.

The way multiple columns work is that PowerPoint will fill the first column completely before it moves on to putting text into the second column. It does not try to balance across your columns, nor does it make an effort to break a column at a bulleted or numbered point.

Since PowerPoint does not have column breaks like Word does, if you want a specific line to start your second column you have to manually make that happen by using Enter to move that line down far enough that it will move over to the second column.

Also, when you add multiple columns they will appear within that designated text box which can sometimes not look great if the text box is too narrow to really support multiple columns.

In some respects adding multiple text boxes to your slide is a better way to have the appearance of multiple columns while being able to better control the appearance of the text on your slide.

Change Spacing Between Lines of Text

If you want to change the amount of space that appears between lines of text, you can do so by clicking into the paragraph you want to change and then going to the Paragraph section of the Home tab and clicking on the arrow next to the Line Spacing option which is in the top row to the right of the increase list level option. It has arrows pointing upward and downward next to a set of lines.

Click on the dropdown arrow to see the available options. As you hold your mouse over each one you'll see what it looks like in the presentation itself. Click on one to select it.

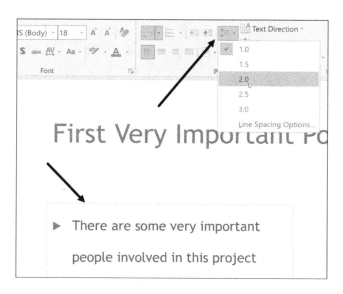

If you choose Line Spacing Options that will bring up the Paragraph dialogue box which can also be opened by right-clicking in the main workspace and choosing Paragraph from the dropdown menu there.

The line spacing options are available in a dropdown in the Spacing section of the dialogue box. In that section of the Paragraph dialogue box you can also change the values for Before and After to place space between your paragraphs.

Here, for example, I've changed the After value to 18 to place a large space between each of these items:

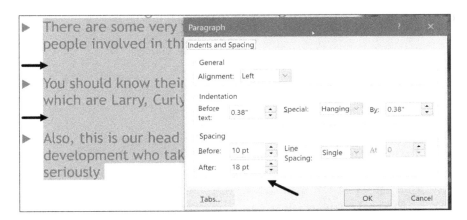

Bulleted Lists

By default, most of the templates include bullets within the main body of each presentation slide. If you want to change the type of bullet, turn off bullets for a specific line, add a bullet to a specific line, or change the bullets to numbers, then you can do so with the Bullets and Numbering options in the top left corner of the Paragraph section of the Home tab.

To change the type of bullet, click on the row you want to change or highlight all of your rows if there's more than one, and then go to the Bullets option (the one with dots next to lines in the top left corner of the Paragraph section of the Home tab) and click on the dropdown arrow.

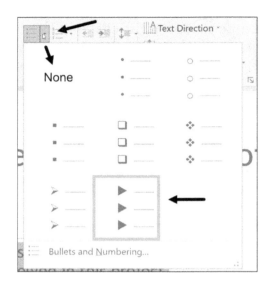

You'll see a box around the type of bullet that's currently being used. Click on None if you don't want a bulleted list. Click on one of the other options if you want to change the type of bullet.

You can hold your cursor over each option to see what it will look like before you make your selection.

Clicking on Bullets and Numbering at the bottom of that list will let you specify the size of the bullet relative to the text as well as the color of the bullet.

If you click on Customize that will let you choose any symbol from the Symbol dialogue box which gives you access to all of the symbols used in fonts like Wingdings which have a number of various shapes available. For example, I was able to change my bullets to a three-leaf clover just now.

The Picture option lets you insert a picture for your bullet.

(But remember that the more you customize things, the more work you have to do throughout your presentation to keep everything uniform and, also, that the you don't want to do something with the formatting of your presentation that distracts from the actual presentation. So, yes, I can in fact make bullets that are pictures of my dog, but that doesn't mean I should.)

Numbered Lists

If you want a numbered or lettered list instead (e.g., 1, 2, 3 or A, B, C) then click on the Numbering dropdown. There you can see a list of available numbered list options to choose from.

If you need to start at a number other than 1 or a letter other than A, click on Bullets and Numbering at the bottom of the list and then choose your starting point using the Start At box in the bottom right.

For lettered lists (A, B, C) when you change that numeric value for Start At it will change the letter. So a 1 equals A, a 2 equals B, etc.

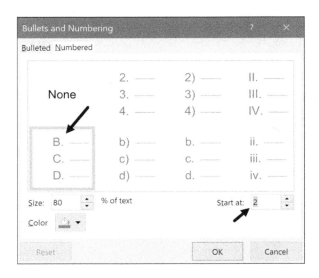

As with the bulleted list, you can also change the relative size of the number or letter compared to the list and change the color of the letter or number using this dialogue box.

Another option for changing both bullets or numbering is to right-click and go to either Bullets or Numbering in the dropdown menu. There is a secondary dropdown that is identical to the one you'll find for each in the Paragraph section of the Home tab.

Format Painter

If you ever find yourself in a situation where the formatting on one section of your presentation or your slide doesn't match another and you don't want to be bothered trying to figure out exactly what the differences are, you can use the Format Painter to copy the formatting from one block of text to another.

This tool can be a lifesaver if someone has done weird things in a presentation you're trying to fix.

To use it, first highlight the text that's formatted the way you want. Next, click on the Format Painter option in the Clipboard section of the Home tab. Then highlight the text that you want to transfer the formatting to.

Font, font size, font color, line spacing, and type of bulleting/numbering should all copy over to the selected text.

You will know that the format painter is on when you see a small paint brush next to your cursor. It will normally turn off the next time you click on text in your presentation, so be sure to go directly to the text you want to transfer the formatting to and highlight all of the text when you do so.

If you have more than one place you want to transfer formatting to, you can double-click on the Format Painter tool and then it will remain on until you turn it back off. To turn it off use the Esc key or click on Format Painter in the Clipboard section of the Home tab once more.

If the result isn't what you wanted or expected use Ctrl + Z to undo it and try again. Sometimes with paragraphs of text it can matter whether you selected the initial paragraph from the top or from the bottom. Same with the paragraph you're transferring the formatting to.

Also, if I want spacing between paragraphs to transfer I always try to select more than one paragraph before I click on the Format Painter.

Add Other Items To a Presentation Slide

Now that we've covered how to add and format text in your presentation let's discuss what other options you have.

If you look at a blank content slide that hasn't had any text added to it yet, you'll see in the center of the text box that there's usually a series of faded images. For example, this is from a text box in a Two Content slide:

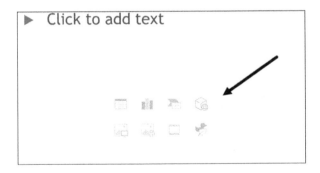

These are the options you have other than just typing text into that box. Your options are Insert Table, Insert Chart, Insert a SmartArt Graphic, 3D Models, Pictures, Online Pictures, Insert Video, and Insert an Icon.

Once you choose one of these options you can't then place text in that area. It's one or the other. (Although you could add a text box to the slide and put in text that way if you wanted. That's intermediate-level so we're not going to cover it here but the option can be found in the Text section of the Insert tab.)

We're not going to cover all of those options in this guide, just adding a table and inserting a picture, but they all work on the same principle and it's good to know they exist.

Alright, then. On to adding a table.

Tables

The first option in that set of images is Insert Table.

Click on it and you'll see the Insert Table dialogue box. It lets you specify the number of columns and rows you want in your table. Below you can see the dialogue box as well as the table that was inserted into the slide using five columns and five rows after I clicked on OK.

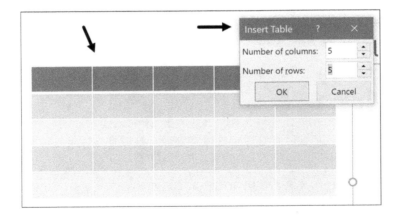

Background Color

By default for this theme, the first row is in a different color because it's a header row for the table. The remaining rows are in alternating colors.

The colors used are consistent with the presentation theme. You can change the colors used in your table under the Table Tools Design tab.

The Table Styles options provide various layouts that use the color palette of the presentation theme. Or you can select all of the cells in the table or a subset of cells, like a row, and use the Shading option to choose a new background color that way.

The Shape Fill option in the mini formatting menu can also be used to change the background color of selected cells.

Font Color

Font color should be set to work with the original background colors. For example on this table the header row uses a white font color but the main body of the table uses a black font color.

That color can be changed on the Home tab or via the mini formatting menu just like any other text. Either select the text you want to change first or make the color change after you click into a cell but before you start typing.

Add Text or Numbers to Your Table

To add information to the table, click into any of the cells in the table and start typing. If you enter text that is wider than the width of the column, it will automatically flow down to another line and the row height will change to make sure all of the text is visible. Like so:

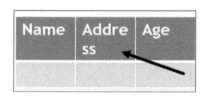

You may need to change your column widths or font size when this happens to better display the text since, as you can see above, having the word "Address" break across that line is not ideal.

If you have your information in an existing table in Word or Excel, you can copy the information from that table into PowerPoint by highlighting the cells in Word or Excel, using copy (Ctrl + C), and then clicking into the first cell in the PowerPoint table where you want to place that information and using paste (Ctrl + V).

If the data you want to paste into your presentation has more columns than the table, PowerPoint will add additional columns. Same with the number of rows. The text in the table will resize to fit on the slide, so it's best to bring in your information first and then format from there.

If you have fewer columns or rows, PowerPoint will just paste your data into the number of columns or rows needed for the data.

PowerPoint is not set up to format numbers well, so I find that it is easier when dealing with numeric data to do that in Excel.

Align Text Within Cells

If after you've entered text into your table you want to change the alignment of the text so that it's centered or left-aligned, etc. you can do this by highlighting the cells you want to change, going to the Table Tools Layout tab, and going to the Alignment section.

The top row where you see the three options with lines is where you can choose to left-align, center, or right-align text. The second row where you see the three boxes with lines in them is where you can choose to place text at the top, center, or bottom of each cell.

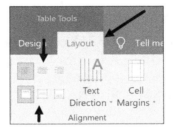

Add Rows or Columns

If you need additional rows in your table, simply use the tab key from the last cell in the last row of the table and PowerPoint will add a new line.

You can also highlight a row, go to the Rows & Columns section of the Table Tools Layout tab, and choose Insert Above or Insert Below.

To add a column, highlight an existing column and choose Insert Left or Insert Right.

You can also highlight a row or column and right-click to bring up the mini formatting menu which has an Insert dropdown with all four choices.

Delete Rows or Columns

To delete a row or column from a table, you can highlight the row or column and use the backspace key. You can also highlight the row or column and then right-click and choose Cut or use the Delete dropdown menu on the mini formatting menu.

Another option is to click into a cell in that row or column, go to the Table Tools Layout tab, and under the Rows & Columns section click on the dropdown arrow under Delete. From there you can choose Delete Columns, Delete Rows, or Delete Table.

Delete the Table

To delete the entire table, right-click on the table and use the Delete option in the mini formatting menu to choose Delete Table.

Or right-click on the table and choose Select Table from the dropdown and then use the Delete or Backspace key.

Or click on the table and then use the Delete dropdown in the Rows & Columns section of the Table Tools Layout tab.

Move the Table

Click on the table to select it. Or right-click and choose Select Table. Hold your mouse over the edge of the table until it looks like a four-sided arrow and then left-click and drag the table to where you want it. Keep in mind that you can drag it on top of another text box but that won't make it part of that text box.

Column Width

To change the width of a column, click on a cell in the column and go to the Cell Size section of the Table Tools Layout tab and change the value for Width. This will change the overall width of the table.

You can also hold your mouse over the right-hand side of the column in the table itself until the cursor looks like two parallel lines with arrows pointing off to the sides and then left-click and drag to your desired width. This will change the width of that column and the one to its right, but not the overall size of the table unless you were resizing the final column in the table.

You can also double-left click along that edge to get the column to automatically resize to the width of the text that's currently in the column. This will also change the width of the table at the same time.

Row Height

To change the height of a row, click on a cell in the row and go to the Cell Size section of Table Tools Layout tab and change the value for Height. You cannot change a row height to a value that would hide any text in that row.

Another option is to hold your mouse over the bottom edge of the row in the table itself until the cursor looks like two parallel lines with arrows pointing up and down and then left-click and drag to your desired height. Once again, you will be limited in how short you can make the row by any existing text in that row and also by the font size for text in that row.

With both methods, only the height of that row will change which means the table height will also change.

Resize the Table

To change the dimensions of an entire table, you can click on the table and then left-click and drag from any of the white circles around the edge of the table. Be sure that you have a white double-sided arrow when you do so or you may just end up moving the table around.

Clicking on one of the white circles in the corner will allow you to resize the table proportionately as long as you click and drag at an angle.

You can also click on the table and go to the Table Tools Layout tab and change the dimensions for the table in the Table Size section.

If you want to resize the table and have the relative height and width of the table stay the same, click the Lock Aspect Ratio box first. When you do that PowerPoint will adjust both measurements at once to keep the ratio of height to width for the table constant.

Split Cells in a Table

You can take one or more cells in a table and split them into multiple cells. To do this, highlight the cell or cells you want to split, go to the Table Tools Layout tab, and click on Split Cells in the Merge section.

This will bring up the Split Cells dialogue box which lets you specify how many columns and rows you want each cell split into.

The choice you make will apply to each cell you selected. So if you select four cells and tell it to split them into two columns and one row, each of those four cells will be split into two columns and one row giving you eight cells total.

You can also bring up the Split Cells dialogue box by right-clicking and choosing Split Cells from the dropdown menu.

Merge Cells in a Table

You can also merge cells in a table which combines the selected cells into one.

In this case, highlight the cells that you want to merge, go to the Table Tools Layout tab, and choose Merge Cells from the Merge section. All of the cells will be combined into one and any text that was in those cells will be shown in the newly-merged cell with one row per line of text working from left to right and top to bottom of the old cell range.

Another option is to select the cells you want to merge, right-click, and choose Merge Cells from the dropdown menu.

Table Design

We already touched on this a bit, but the Table Tools Design tab will let you control the appearance of your table.

You can change the borders around and within your table using the Borders dropdown. Before you apply a border be sure to change the line width, style, and color in the Draw Borders section if you want those settings to be different from the default settings..

Also, the Table Style Options section will let you turn on or off banded rows in your table. (This is where each row of the table has an alternating color.)

You can also turn on or off banded columns which applies alternating colors to each column.

I do not recommend having alternating rows and alternating columns on at the same time.

In the Table Style Options section you can also adjust the settings so that the last row (total row), first column, or last column are formatted differently by checking the boxes for those options.

Pictures

The option directly below Insert Table is Pictures. Click on it and you'll see the Insert Picture dialogue box. By default it will open in your Pictures folder on your computer, but you can navigate from there to any location where the picture you want is stored.

If you click on the All Pictures dropdown option next to the File Name box you can see the picture file types that PowerPoint will accept. (Which looks to be pretty much any type you can image.)

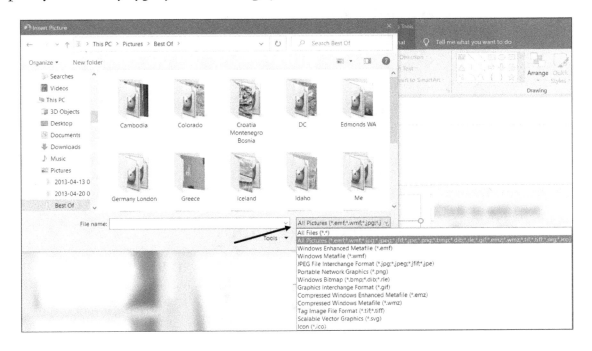

Navigate to where the picture you want is saved, click on the picture, and then choose Insert. This will insert that picture into that text box. It will be centered.

You can also click on the arrow next to Insert and choose to link your photo instead, but I'd generally advise against that because it's far too easy to break a link like that. For example, you link to an image and then copy your presentation to a thumb drive so you can use it on the provided laptop at the conference center and suddenly there are no images in your presentation and you're standing in front of five hundred people not knowing why. (Or knowing why but also knowing it's too late to fix it.)

Better usually to just put the image into your presentation. The reasons to link instead of insert are if you think the image may be updated at some point outside of PowerPoint or if you are using a large number of images and need to keep the file size down. For a printed presentation it won't be a problem. For a presentation you're presenting be sure you have access to those images at the time of your presentation.

Okay, then.

The image you chose will insert into your slide at a size that fits within the text box where you chose to insert it. If the image is smaller than the active area it will insert at its current size, but if it's larger than the active area it will be scaled down.

(This is for when you use the Pictures icon to insert an image into a text box. You can also go to the Insert tab and choose Pictures from the Images section there to insert a picture on a blank slide. In that case the image you insert will be centered in the presentation slide and may fit the entire slide if it's large enough.)

Now let's discuss what you can do with a picture you've inserted into your presentation.

Move a Picture

To move your image, left-click on it and drag it to the location you want. (It will take the text box it was inserted into with it, but if you then delete the image, the text box will reappear in its original location.)

Resize a Picture

You can also resize a picture after you insert it into your slide. If you have specific dimensions that you want to use, click on the image and go to the Picture Tools Format tab. At the far end you'll see the Size section.

Change either the height or the width and the image will resize proportionately, meaning that PowerPoint will adjust the other measurement to keep the height to width ratio the same. This is a good thing because it prevents the image from becoming distorted or skewed.

You can also click onto the image and then left-click on any of the white circles around the perimeter and drag until the image is the size you want. This will not resize the image proportionately, so you can easily end up with a distorted image if you do it this way. But if you click on a corner and drag at an angle that usually will keep the height and width proportional because you are resizing the image on both dimensions at once. (If you don't like the result, use Ctrl + Z to undo.)

Another option is to right-click on the image and choose Size and Position. This will open a Format Picture task pane on the right-hand side of your workspace, which includes fields for Height and Width. You can uncheck the Lock Aspect Ratio box if you want to change one measure independent of the other.

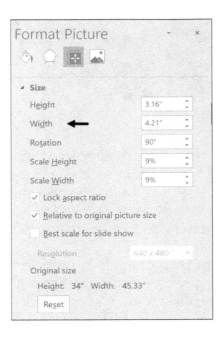

Also, you can reset the image to its original appearance from here, but be careful because that will remove the settings PowerPoint applied to the image as well. So if it resized it to fit that text box or changed the image orientation, that will be lost too.

The Format Picture task pane can also be accessed by clicking on the expansion arrow in the Size section of the Picture Tools Format tab.

Rotate a Picture

If you want to rotate the picture that you inserted, click on the image and then click on the little white outline of an arrow circling to the right that will be visible along the edge or top of the image.

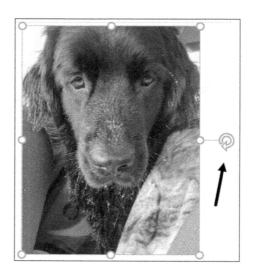

Click and hold this while you move your cursor in the direction you want to rotate the image and it will rotate along with your mouse.

Your other option is to click on the image and then go to the Picture Tools Format tab and click on the dropdown arrow next to Rotate in the Arrange section.

You can choose from there to rotate the image 90 degrees right or left or flip the image vertically or horizontally.

If you need more options than that, click on More Rotation Options to bring up the Format Picture task pane on the right-hand side of the screen. Rotation is the third option in the Size section. You can click into the box there and set the rotation to any value you want from 1 degree to 360 degrees.

(Technically it lets you set a value from -3600 degrees to 3600 degrees, but a circle is only 360 degrees, so…)

Crop a Picture

Sometimes I'll drop a picture into a presentation and then realize that I didn't want the entire picture, I just wanted a section of it. (This is especially true when I take screenshots of Excel using Print Screen and then want to just keep a small section of that screenshot for my presentation.) In those cases, I need to crop the image to only show the portion I care about.

To crop an image, right-click on the image and choose Crop from the mini formatting bar. You should then see small black bars on each side of the image and at the corners. Be sure when you click and drag that the cursor looks like a bar, because otherwise you might end up resizing the image instead. (If so, Ctrl + Z to undo and try again.)

Left-click on those bars and drag until only the portion of the image that you want to keep is fully visible. (The area that will be cropped away will be grayed out but still partially visible like bottom portion of the image below.)

To permanently apply the crop to your image, click away or hit Esc.

If you start to crop your image and realize that you want a different portion of the image in the visible area, you can click and drag on the image to move it around. The part that will remain after you finish will still be fully visible but the rest will be grayed out.

This is especially useful if you insert an image and PowerPoint crops the image for you, because it doesn't always know what part of the image you want visible. Choosing to crop but not actually doing so will let you move that image around until the portion of the image you want visible is in the active area.

Your other option for cropping is to go to the Picture Tools Format tab and choose Crop from the Size section. The first option in the dropdown is a simple crop.

For an image that's already been cropped, the full image will appear with the cropped space already marked. This makes it relatively easy to fix the cropping of an image if you get it wrong the first time since you can just choose to crop again and then drag the image or the bars to the correct location.

In the Crop dropdown in the Picture Tools Format tab you also have the option to crop to a shape or crop to a specific aspect ratio but those are more advanced options that we're not going to cover here.

Bring Forward/Send Backward

If you are ever in a situation where you have images or text boxes that overlap (which if you're using a standard template would only happen if you moved something around), you may need to use the bring forward or send backward options.

Visualize the layers of text and images in your presentation as a stack of playing cards. You're only going to see what's visible from the top of the stack. Which means if you shuffle those cards into a different order, you will see something different.

So, for example, if you have a layer with a picture that you want to be in the background of a layer with text, then you would want to place the picture layer behind the text layer. You could do this by using one of the Send Backward options to position the layer with the picture behind the layer with text.

You could get the same result by using one of the Bring Forward options on the text layer.

The Bring Forward and Send Backward options are available in the Arrange section of the Picture Tools Format tab. There is a dropdown for each one.

Send Backward has the choice to Send Backward, which will move a layer back one spot, or to Send to Back, which will make that layer the bottom layer.

Bring Forward has the option to Bring Forward, which will move a layer up one spot, or Bring to Front, which will make it the topmost layer.

The Bring Forward and Send Backward options are also available by right-clicking on an image and choosing them from the dropdown menu.

I should note here that sometimes Bring Forward and Send Backward didn't perform the way I expected them to, but Bring to Front and Send to Back always did. So if you get stuck with that issue as well, you should be able to stack your layers in any order you want by strategically applying the Bring to Front and Send to Back options. Not as easy, but it works.

Alignment

You can align images to one another or you can align them with respect to the presentation slide itself. If you're using a template and bringing in images as part of a text box, you shouldn't really need to use this, but the option does exist under the Align option in the Arrange section of the Picture Tools Format tab.

You can choose to align left (place the image along the left-hand side of the slide), align center (place the image in the center of the slide as judged from left to right), align right (place the image along the right-hand side of the slide), align top (place the image along the top edge of the slide), align middle (place the image in the center of the slide as judged from top to bottom), or align bottom (place the image along the bottom edge of the slide).

Distribute horizontally will center the image judged from left to right. Distribute vertically will center the image judged from top to bottom. Where this one matters is when you have multiple images selected at once. If you have multiple images selected at once then it will take those images and distribute them either across the width of the slide (horizontally) or from top to bottom (vertically) so that there is equal space between the images and the edges of the slide.

If you do have multiple images, you can select those images, and then under Align choose Align Selected Objects and instead of aligning the objects to the presentation slide it will align them to one another. So, for example, align right would move the left-hand object into alignment with the right-hand object.

Picture Styles

There is a Picture Styles section in the Picture Tools Format tab. Most of the styles involve placing a frame around the image, but some of them also involve skewing the image or adding a shadow to the image so that it looks three-dimensional.

To apply a picture style, click on your image and go the Picture Styles section of the Picture Tools Format tab. Hold your mouse over each style to see what it will look like when applied to your image. Click on one if you want to actually apply it.

Adjust a Picture

PowerPoint provides a number of options for adjusting an image. As with most things, I will advise you against getting too out of control with the special effects. There are industries where that may be warranted, but most times you want to present your information in as clear and succinct a way as possible.

Having said that, click on an image and then go to the Picture Tools Format tab and you'll see on the far left-hand side that there is a section called Adjust.

The Corrections option will allow you to sharpen or soften an image as well as adjust the brightness/contrast of the image.

The Color option will allow you to change the saturation or tone of your image as well as recolor your image.

Artistic Effects allows you to adjust your image so that it looks like a marker drawing, pencil sketch, etc.

For all three options, click on the dropdown arrow to see how each choice will impact your image.

(As a side note, if you really need to do something like this I'd recommend using an image software program instead and then bringing in the already-edited image but I do know that some people do design work in PowerPoint itself. This is where you'd go to do so.)

Animations

If you have a presentation slide with multiple bullet points it's often very useful to have those bullet points appear one at a time. This way people listen to what you're saying instead of trying to read ahead on the slide and see what you're going to say next.

To do this, first go to the slide where you want to add animation. Next, click on the first line of text that you want to have appear and go to the Animations tab. Click on one of the options in the Animation section.

I recommend using Appear. It simply shows the line without any fancy tricks which can be distracting.

Once you apply animation to one bulleted point in your slide, PowerPoint will apply it to the remainder of the items in your slide.

The order in which those items will appear is shown by the way they are numbered. All items numbered 1 will appear first, then all items numbered 2, then all items numbered 3, etc.

So in the example below we have three bulleted items, each of which will appear one at a time starting with the top bullet.

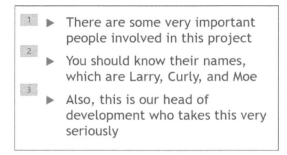

The appearance of the next item is usually triggered by hitting Enter, using the down arrow on your keyboard, or left-clicking to advance through the slide as you present.

If you have indented lines of text, so sub-bullets, you will probably need to fix their numbering because by default they will appear at the same time as their "parent" line.

This is probably best understood visually. See below:

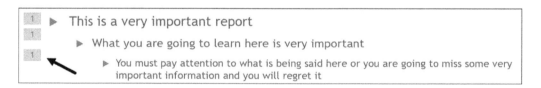

All three lines of text in the image above have a 1 next to them. That means they're all going to appear together which I generally do not want because that means my audience will be reading ahead instead of listening to me.

To fix this, click into the slide, go to the Animations tab and click on the expansion arrow for the Animation section.

This will bring up the Appear dialogue box.

In that dialogue box, click on the Text Animation tab, which is the third one. There will be a dropdown option at the top labeled Group Text. Click on that and choose one of the other grouping levels.

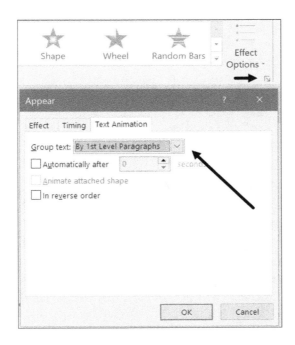

Depending on how many levels of bullets you have on the slide you will probably need the "By 2nd Level Paragraphs" or the "By 3rd Level Paragraphs" option to get all lines of text to appear individually. Once you've made your choice, click on OK.

The slide will now show adjusted numbering based upon your choice. With 3rd Level Paragraphs that means the first three level of bullets are treated as separate lines that appear one at a time instead of grouped together.

By default, a picture will appear when the slide appears. If instead you want your picture to appear after your text, then you need to also apply animation to the picture. You do so the same way you would with your text by clicking on an animation choice in the Animation tab.

If the picture is the first item you applied animation to it will be numbered 1. If you apply animation to it after you apply animation to your text, it will be set to appear after all of your text.

To change the order in which your different elements appear on the slide, go to the Animations tab and click on Animation Pane in the Advanced Animation section.

This will bring up the Animation Pane task pane, which will show all of your elements and the order in which they appear.

(You may have to click on the small double arrow under a numbered section to see all of your numbered options from your slide. In the image above I've already done that so clicking on it again would hide them.)

To change the order of your elements, click on one of the elements listed and then use the up and down arrows at the top to move that element up or down.

You can also change the level at which your text is grouped in this pane by clicking on the arrow next to one of the text elements and then choosing Effect Options from the dropdown menu.

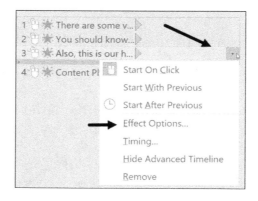

That will bring up the Appear dialogue box.

If you want to have some of your bullet points appear together but others appear separately, the best way I know to do this is to set up the slide as if everything will appear separately and then highlight the rows you want to have appear together and click on your chosen animation option once more. This will change the numbering of those items so that they all are grouped together.

There are other things you can do with animation that we're not going to cover here, such as have each bullet point appear on its own on a timed schedule. But for this beginner guide I just wanted you to know how to structure your slides so that each point you want to make appears separately.

If you click on the downward-pointing arrow with a line under it to expand the animations box you'll see that there is actually a variety of animation choices. Some animations are for bringing in text or images, some are for emphasizing what's already there, and some are for taking it away. The different categories are color-coded with green for entrance, yellow for emphasis, and red for exit.

You can see what each animation will look like by applying it. It will automatically run once when you do so. If it doesn't or you want to see it again later, click on the Preview option in the left-hand corner of the Animations tab and your animations for that slide should re-run.

I know it's tempting to try to make a presentation more interesting with things like this, but if you can't engage your audience with what you're saying then fix what you're saying instead.

I would strongly urge you to keep to just using Appear as your animation option. You can absolutely have your bullet points fly in or even bounce in (please, no), but ask yourself if that's appropriate for your audience.

If you're presenting to first graders, sure, have a bullet point bounce in. But a potential business client? Eh. Or a group of your professional peers? Uh-uh. Don't do it. Don't fall for the temptation.

Okay since we're talking about how to make a presentation "professional", let's talk about a few design principles to keep in mind as well while we're at it.

Design Principles

I've touched on this a few times, but I think it's good to take a chapter and discuss some basic design principles to keep in mind as you're preparing your presentation. I'm going to assume here that you're actually intending to use your PowerPoint presentation as a presentation. Meaning, you're going to talk through it and not expect it to talk for you, and that the slides are going to be presented on a projector of some sort to a live audience.

(In other words, I'm not addressing the consulting model of using PowerPoint where you put together a weekly client presentation on a series of slides that you hand out to your client and pack full of information and then walk through even though the client could just read the darned things themselves without paying you thousands of dollars for you to be there while they do it.)

Font Size

Make sure that all of the text on your slide will be visible to anyone in the room. I'd try to have all of the text be 14 point or larger if you can manage it.

Font Type

As with all other design elements it can be tempting to use a fancy font. Resist the temptation. You want a basic, clear, easy-to-read font for your presentation elements. This means using something like Arial or Calibri or Times New Roman instead of something like Algerian.

Summaries Instead of Explanations

The text on your slide should be there as a general outline of what you're going to say, not contain the full text of what you want to say. Think of each bullet point as a prompt that you can look at to trigger your recollection.

The reason you do it this way is because people will try to read whatever you put in front of them. So if you give them a slide full of text they will be busy reading that text rather than listening to what you have to say.

Also, if it's all on the slide, why listen to you at all?

So use the text on your slide as a high-level summary of your next point instead of as an explanation.

For example, I might have a slide titled "The Three Stages of Money Laundering" and then list on that slide three bullet points, "Placement", "Layering", and "Integration". As I show each bullet point I'll discuss what each of those stages is and how it works. If I feel a need to really go into detail then I'll have a separate slide for each one where I provide further information in small bite-sized chunks.

Contrast

You want your text to be visible. Which means you have to think about contrast. If you have a dark background, then use a light-colored text. For example, dark blue background, white text. If you have a light background, use a dark-colored text. For example, white background, black text.

And beware of anything that could trip up someone with color-blindness. So no red on green or green on red and no blue on yellow or yellow on blue.

Also, and this may be more of a personal preference, but I try to use the slide templates that have white for the background behind the text portions of my slides. I'm fine with colorful borders and colorful header sections, but where the meat of the presentation is I prefer to have a white background often with black text. (That's the easiest combination to read.)

So I'll choose the Ion Boardroom theme before I'll choose the Ion theme, for example.

Don't Get Cute

PowerPoint has a lot of bells and whistles. You can have lines of text that fly in and slide in and fade away. Or slides that flash in or appear through bars. And some of the templates it provides are downright garish.

Resist the urge to overdo it.

Ask yourself every time you're tempted to add some special effect if adding it will improve the effectiveness of your presentation. And ask yourself what your boss's boss's boss would think of your presentation. I've worked in banking and regulatory environments and I will tell you there is little appreciation in those environments for overly-bright colors and flashy special effects. (Whereas some tech company environment where the CEO wears jeans and t-shirts to work may be all for that kind of thing. Know your audience.)

I do think that using the animation option to have one bullet point appear at a time is a good idea. But you can do that with the Appear option. You don't need Fade, Fly In, Float In, Split, Wipe, etc.

And, yes, it can sometimes feel boring to use the same animation for a hundred slides in a row. But remember the point of your presentation is to convey information to your audience. Anything that doesn't help you do that should go.

Other Tips and Tricks

Now that we've walked through the basics of creating your presentation, let's cover a few other things you might want to do, starting with adding notes to your slides.

Add Notes To A Slide

If you add notes to your slides you can then print a notes version of those slides that lets you see not just the slide that your audience sees but any additional comments. So if you're worried about forgetting something but don't want too much text on your slide? Put it in a note.

There is also a display option that lets you see the notes on your screen but not have them appear to the audience. Either one is a great option when you have points you want to be sure to make but don't want to clutter up your slides.

To use notes, though, you first have to add them.

The Notes portion of the presentation is not visible by default, but if you look at the bottom middle of your workspace you should see a little item that says Notes. Click on that and a task pane that says "Click to add notes" will open below your slide.

Click there and start typing to add your notes.

The other option to open or close the Notes task pane is to go to the Show section of the View tab and click on Notes. If the task pane was already open it will close, if it wasn't it will appear.

Spellcheck

It's always a good idea to run spellcheck on anything you create for an audience. To check the spelling in your document, go to the Proofing section of the Review tab and click on Spelling. (It's on the far left-hand side.)

PowerPoint will then walk through your entire document flagging spelling errors and repeated words.

If there are no errors you'll see a dialogue box that tells you the spell check is complete. Click OK to close it.

If there are errors, the Spelling task pane will open and for each one PowerPoint will show a suggested change and highlight the word it flagged in the slide itself. For example, here I had the word "is" twice in a row:

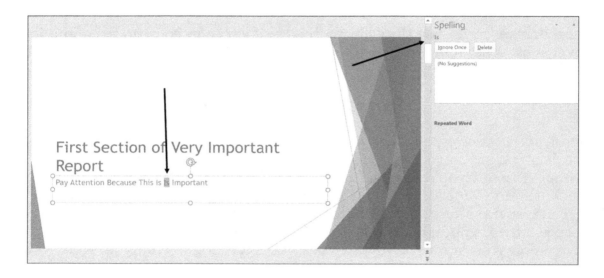

If you don't want to make the suggested change, click on Ignore.

For spelling errors PowerPoint will give you the choice to Ignore All or to Ignore Once. Ignore Once when you just want it to skip this one instance; Ignore All when you want it to skip the word everywhere it occurs in the presentation. For example, I often have to tell Office programs to ignore my first name because it almost always flags it as a spelling error.

That does bring up the third option you'll get with a spelling error which is Add. This will add the word to your version of PowerPoint's dictionary so that the word is never flagged as a spelling error again. So if there's some term that's common to your industry but not in the PowerPoint dictionary you can add the word and then it won't be flagged in any of your presentations. In contrast, Ignore All just applies to the current presentation.

For any issues it flags, PowerPoint will suggest solutions, like above where it gave the option to delete the duplicate word. Click on that option to apply the solution.

With spelling errors, if it can identify a close enough word it will suggest alternatives like here where I misspelled "regret" as "regert" and it suggested four possible words I might have meant.

To replace the current word with one of the suggestions, click on the suggested word and then click on Change to change this one instance or Change All to change all uses of the misspelled word in the document.

Be careful with Change All and Ignore All. It's possible to miss an error by using one of those options. Also, spellcheck is not infallible. There are times when I've spelled a word wrong but it created another word that was in the dictionary and so PowerPoint didn't flag it. (I really do wish they had spellcheck for certain lowkey cusswords since at least one seems to be pretty easy to use inadvertently.) A good reminder to always read your presentation when you're done. Technology can only do so much.

Find

If you need to find a specific reference in your slides you can use Find to do so. The Find option is in the Editing section of the Home tab (on the far right-hand side). Click on Find and the Find dialogue box will appear.

You can also open the Find dialogue box by using Ctrl + F.

Type the word you want into the white text box under "Find What" and then click on Find Next. PowerPoint will walk you through the entire document moving to the next instance of that word each time you click on Find Next.

You can sometimes save time by choosing to just search for whole words only or to just search for words with the same capitalization (match case). For example, in my industry CAT is a term that is used at times for consolidated audit trail. When I want to find that term in a presentation I match case and find whole words only so I don't have to wade through words like catastrophe or catalog.

Replace Text

If you need to replace text within your slides you can use Replace. This essentially pairs the Find option with an option that takes the word you were searching for and replaces it with another. You can either launch the Replace dialogue box by using Ctrl + H or by going to the Editing section of the Home tab and clicking on Replace.

When you do this you'll see the Replace dialogue box.

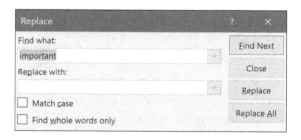

The "Find what" box is what you are looking for. The "Replace with" box is what you want to put in its place.

The match case and find whole words only options are helpful when using Find but essential when using Replace. I have seen more than one very awkward instance of replace that went wrong. For example, I mentioned above that CAT is a term I might search for. Think what would happen if I replaced all instances of "cat" with "consolidated audit trail" including in the word catalog.

For replace you can replace your instances of a word one at a time by using the Replace option or you can replace them all at once using Replace All. Be careful with this. And be sure to read the whole presentation if you use Replace All.

Replacing text is easy to do and easy to mess up.

Replace Font

If you go to the Editing section of the Home tab and click on the dropdown arrow next to Replace you'll see that there is an option there to Replace Fonts.

Click on that option to bring up the Replace Font dialogue box. It will show you two dropdown menus.

The first dropdown is where you select the font that is in your presentation that you want to replace. It should only show the fonts used in your presentation. (But don't worry if it shows one or two you didn't think you were using. They may be used somewhere you can't see.)

The second dropdown is where you choose the font you want to replace it with.

Once you've selected both fonts, click on Replace and every usage of the first font will be replaced with the second font. This can come in very handy if you have a corporate requirement to use a specific font that wasn't followed when the presentation was created. (Ask me how I know…)

Just be sure to then look back through your presentation and make sure everything looks "right", because different fonts take up different amounts of space. It's possible that changing over the font could impact the appearance of your slides.

Presentation Size

PowerPoint gives you the choice between two presentation sizes. The standard size is 4:3 and the widescreen size is 16:9. You can also choose a custom slide size.

All of these choices are available in the Customize section of the Design tab on the far right side where it says Slide Size. Click on the dropdown arrow to make your choice.

(If you click on the Custom Slide Size option you can even make a presentation that is in portrait orientation, so like a normal printed report, rather than in landscape orientation. Although, if you're going to do this do it before you start putting together your slides or you'll have a complete mess to fix up. This would not be a good choice for a presentation that's going to be projected on a screen, but could be an interesting idea for a printed presentation.)

Present Your Slides

When it comes time to do your presentation, chances are someone will hook up a laptop with your presentation on it to a projector. By default that will show your computer screen. But you don't want someone to see what you've been seeing this whole time as you built your presentation. You just want them to see the slides and nothing else.

Which means you need to go into presentation mode.

To do this, go to the Slide Show tab. On the left-hand side you have the Start Slide Show section. If you click on From Beginning, this will start a presentation at the first slide in your PowerPoint presentation. If you click on From Current Slide it will start the presentation at the slide that's currently visible.

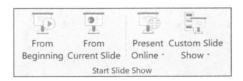

F5 will also start your presentation from the beginning. And Shift + F5 will start your presentation from your current slide.

Either choice will launch the slides you've created as a full-screen presentation.

There are a number of ways to navigate through your presentation. You can use Enter, left-click, page down, or the down arrow to move to the next slide or bullet point. You can use page up or the up arrow to move to the previous slide or bullet point.

You can also right-click and choose Next or Previous from the dropdown menu.

The PowerPoint screen you've been working in will still be there and open behind the scenes. You can reach it using Alt + Tab to move through your active windows or you can use Esc to close the presentation.

Before you enter presentation mode, I'd recommend having any additional windows you're going to want open already so you can easily access them using Alt + Tab.

And it's always a good idea to run through your presentation slides before you present to anyone so you can check and make sure that all the animations, etc. are working.

There is an option to view your slides in Presenter View. What this does is show on your computer screen the slide the audience can currently see as well as your slide notes and the next slide, but on the presentation screen only the presentation slide will show.

Because I'm currently using both an external monitor and my laptop, when I launch a presentation this happens automatically.

If you don't want that, you can go to the presenter screen and in Display settings change it to Duplicate Slide View. This will make it so both screens just show the presentation

If you need to switch which screen shows which information, choose Swap Presenter View and Slide Show. (Just be aware that if you do this in front of a live audience and you're using notes that they will see any notes you have.)

You can also show and hide presenter view by right-clicking on your presentation and choosing that option from the dropdown.

To close a presentation, hit Esc. Or, right-click and choose End Show from the dropdown menu.

That's the basics of presenting. There are more advanced options, like setting up your slides to advance on a schedule, that are more advanced topics.

Print Your Presentation

You have the option to print your presentation slides, your presentation slides as handouts (so with room for people to take notes), or your presentation slides with your notes.

To do any of these, type Ctrl + P or go to the File tab and then choose Print on the left-hand side.

Both choices will bring you to the Print screen.

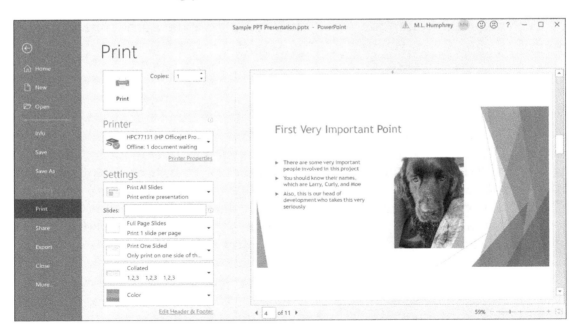

On the left-hand side are your File tab choices, next you'll see a printer icon with a number of setting choices below that, and then on the right-hand side will be a preview of the current slide. You can use the numbers and arrows below that to navigate between your slides.

The default is to print all of your slides and in full-page format and that's what your preview will show. But let's walk through everything you can see on this page and your other possible print options.

Print

Right at the top of the page under the Print header is the printer icon. It shows a printer and says Print under it. This is what you click when you're ready to print your document.

Copies

Next to that is where you specify the number of copies to print. By default the number to print is 1, but you can use the arrows on the right-hand side of the text box to increase that number. (Or decrease it if you've already increased it.) You can also just click into the white text box and type the number of copies you want.

Printer

Below those two options is the Printer section. This is where you specify the printer to use. It should be your default printer, but in some corporate environments you'll want to change your printer choice if, for example, you need the color printer.

To do this, click on the arrow on the right-hand side. This will bring up a dropdown menu with all of your printers listed. Click on the one you want. If the one you want isn't listed then use Add Printer to add it.

Printer Properties

You can click on the text that says Printer Properties right below that although most of the options covered there will also be covered in the Settings section on the main page. If you do click, the Paper/Quality tab this is where you can choose the type of paper, its source, and the quality of your print job.

Print All Slides/Print Selection/Print Current Slide/ Custom Range

Your next option is what to print. By default, you'll print all the slides in the presentation.

If you were clicked onto a specific slide in the presentation and want to just print it then you can choose Print Current Slide. (When you choose this the print preview should change to show just that one slide.)

If you had selected more than one slide in the presentation and then chose to print, you can choose Print Selection to print those slides. (You'd do that in the left-hand task pane.)

Your other option is to print a custom range. The easiest way to use this one is to type the slide numbers you want into the Slides text box directly below the dropdown. This will automatically change the dropdown selection to Custom Range. Your preview will also change to just show the slides you've listed.

You can list numbers either individually or as ranges. If you list a range you use a dash between the first and last number. So 1-10 would print slides 1 through 10. You can also use commas to separate numbers or ranges. So 1, 2, 5-12 would print slides 1, 2 and 5 through 12.

Full Page Slides/Notes Pages/Outline/Handouts

The next choice is what you want to print.

In the top section you can choose to print full page slides, notes pages, or an outline.

Full page slides will put one slide on each page you print and nothing else.

Notes pages will put one slide per page on the top half of the page and your notes on the bottom half of the page. Each page will be in portrait orientation. (Short edge on the top.)

The Outline option will take all of the text from your slides and list it out in the same way it's listed on the slides. So if there are bullet points, the outline will have them, too. If there aren't, it won't. Each printed page will contain multiple slides' worth of information. No images are included.

If you want to provide handout slides the next section gives you a number of options to choose from.

The one slide option will center each presentation slide in the middle of a page in portrait orientation. (Not recommended.) The two slide option will put two slides on each page in portrait orientation. (This is a good choice for handouts because it's still visible but doesn't waste paper the way the one-slide option does.)

You can put as many as nine slides on the page, but before you do that think about how legible that will be for the end-user. If you have a lot of slides with images it might be fine, but if they have a lot of text on them or if people will need/want to take a lot of notes, no one is going to thank you for putting nine slides on a page.

The horizontal and vertical choices determine whether the slides are ordered across and then down (horizontal) or down and then across (vertical). I think, at least in the U.S., that most people would expect horizontal.

Print One Sided/Print On Both Sides

If you want to print on both sides of the page this is where you would specify that. The default is to just print on one side of the page, but you can choose to print on both sides and either flip on the short edge or the long edge of the page.

If the paper orientation is Portrait, choose Flip on Long Edge. If the paper orientation is Landscape, choose Flip on Short Edge. For presentation slides you'll generally be working in landscape and want to flip on the short edge, but if you're printing handouts or with notes you'll generally want portrait and to flip on the long edge.

Collated/Uncollated

This only matters if you're printing more than one copy of the presentation. In that case, you need to decide if you want to print one full copy at a time x number of times (collated) or if you want to print x copies of page 1 and then x copies of page 2 and then x copies of page 3 and so on until you've printed all pages of your document (uncollated).

In general, I would recommend collated, which is also the default. In most situations I've been in the audience is given the entire presentation at the start. But if you're handing out the presentation slides one at a time then uncollated will make that easier to do.

Portrait Orientation/Landscape Orientation

This determines whether what you've chosen to print prints with the long edge of the page at the top (landscape) or the short end of the page at the top (portrait).

In general, PowerPoint chooses this for you and does a good job of it. For example, outline should be portrait and full page slides should be landscape and PowerPoint makes that adjustment for you.

However, you might want to change this for the handout slides. For one slide, four slide, and nine slide printing, I think landscape is a better choice than portrait. You can judge for yourself by looking at the preview and seeing how large the slides are and how much white space is taken up with each orientation.

Color/Grayscale/Pure Black and White

This option lets you choose whether to print your slides in color or not. The choice you make will probably depend on your available print resources. When you change the option you'll see in the print preview what each one looks like.

The Color option will look just like your slides:

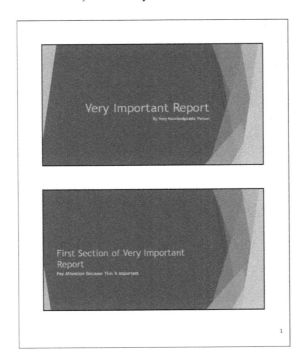

The Grayscale option will print your background elements but strips out any solid background color and converts any colors on the page and any images to grayscale.

The pure black and white one looks to strip the background color as well as the color from most of the design elements. It does appear to leave images in the main body of the presentation in grayscale.

Edit Header & Footer

At the very bottom of the list you can click on the Edit Header & Footer text to bring up the Header and Footer dialogue box where you can choose to add headers or footers to your printed document. The choices available to you will depend on what you're printing.

There are separate tabs for Slides and for Notes and Handouts.

For Slides you can add the date and time, a slide number, and a footer. There is an option to not show this information for the title slide.

For Notes and Handouts you can add the date and time, page number, a header, and a footer.

Some templates will include headers and footers by default.

Once you make your choices, you can see how it will look in the print preview.

Where to Look For Other Answers

Okay, so that's what we're going to cover in this introductory guide.

My goal was to give you a solid understanding of how PowerPoint works and to lead you through the basics of creating a presentation.

There are a number of topics I didn't cover in this guide, such as how to change a presentation slide background color, creating a custom design template, adding timing to your presentation slides, adding objects or text boxes to a slide, adding charts, etc.

At some point you'll probably want to learn about one of those things.

So how do you do it? Where do you get these answers?

First, in PowerPoint itself you have a few options. You can hold your cursor over the choices in any of the tabs and you'll usually see a brief explanation of what that choice can do.

If that brief description isn't enough, a lot of the options have a Tell Me More option below that, like here for the New Slide option in the Insert tab.

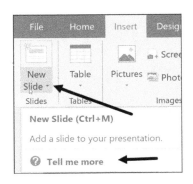

Click on Tell Me More and the built-in Help function in PowerPoint will open a task pane that provides a more detailed discussion of that option. In this example it opens a help topic titled "Add, rearrange, duplicate, and delete slides in PowerPoint" that includes a video as well as written instructions.

Another option is to go directly to the built-in Help function. You do this by clicking on the Help tab and then choosing Help again. You can also press F1.

This will open the Help task pane and you can either search for what you need or navigate through the menu options from there.

I sometimes need more information than this so turn to the internet. (More so with Word and Excel than PowerPoint, but it happens sometimes.)

If I need to know the mechanics of how something works, the Microsoft website is the best option. For example, if I wanted to understand more about the colors used in each theme in PowerPoint I might search for "colors powerpoint theme microsoft 2019".

It's key that you add the powerpoint, microsoft, and your version year in your search so that the result is relevant to your situation.

When I get my search results, I then look for a search result that goes to support.office.com. There will usually be one in the top three or four search results.

If that doesn't work or I need to know something that isn't about how things work but whether something is possible, then I will do an internet search to find a blog or user forum where someone else had the same question. Often there are good tutorials out there that you can read or watch to find your answer.

And, of course, you can also just reach out to me at mlhumphreywriter@gmail.com and I'll try to help if I can.

I'm happy to track down an answer for you or point you in the right direction. Although don't ask me to do your presentation for you. That I won't do. Or I'll do it, but I'll bill you for it.

Conclusion

So there you have it. We've covered the basics of PowerPoint and at this point in time you should be able to create your own nicely polished basic presentation.

Knowing how to create a presentation like this is a valuable skill. I've used PowerPoint presentations for small groups all the way up to rooms full of five hundred people. When you're suddenly standing in front of an audience a presentation like this can help keep you organized and focused on what you wanted to say. It also keeps you from forgetting some vital point as everyone in the room stares at you.

And having a presentation to refer to will in general make you a better presenter because you won't be staring down at a pile of notes the entire time. It also gives your audience something to look at other than you.

Just a final reminder, keep your audience in mind when creating a presentation. Most of my presentations have been given in corporate or regulatory settings, some in more creative settings. But I always live by the motto that the presentation is there to support me not distract from what I'm saying which is why I keep all the crazy shapes and garish color combinations to a minimum. (Although, even I have my weaknesses as you saw with me using the picture of my dog in this book.)

Anyway. Good luck with it. And reach out if you get stuck.

And if you want to continue to learn more about PowerPoint, check out *PowerPoint 2019 Intermediate*.

PowerPoint 2019 Intermediate

POWERPOINT ESSENTIALS 2019 BOOK 2

M.L. HUMPHREY

CONTENTS

CONTENTS (CONT.)

Introduction

In *PowerPoint 2019 Beginner* we covered the basics of what you need to know to use PowerPoint 2019. That book focused on the core knowledge you need to navigate and use PowerPoint with an emphasis on using Microsoft's templates rather than trying to create a presentation from scratch.

While there was discussion of basic text formatting and how to present your slides, the emphasis was on letting PowerPoint do most of the work for you and keeping things simple.

Now in *PowerPoint 2019 Intermediate* we're going to take that base of knowledge and expand upon it by covering subjects such as how to add charts to a presentation, how to work with SmartArt and WordArt, adding equations, symbols, and shapes to a presentation, inserting videos and online photos, using slide transitions, and how to save presentations as PDFs or images.

We won't cover every single thing you can do in PowerPoint, but we'll get close.

And, as always, I will probably share a few opinions along the way since PowerPoint is the program I think is most prone to horrid abuse by those who value whirring and spinning special effects over a simple and straight-forward presentation of good content.

Alright then. With that said, let's get started with a refresh on basic terminology. (Keep in mind that if you're brand new to PowerPoint you may want to start with *PowerPoint 2019 Beginner* instead because I'm going to assume you already know what was covered there and skip past it quickly if it does come up.)

Basic Terminology Recap

Before we begin, I want to make sure that you know what I'm referring to when I say certain things.

Tab

I refer to the menu choices at the top of the screen (File, Home, Insert, Design, Transitions, Animations, Slide Show, Review, View, and Help) as tabs.

Click

If I tell you to click on something, that means to use your mouse (or trackpad) to move the arrow on the screen over to a specific location and left-click or right-click on the option.

If you left-click, this selects the item. If you right-click, this generally creates a dropdown list of options to choose from. If I don't tell you which to do, left- or right-click, then left-click.

Select or Highlight

If I tell you to select text, that means to left-click at the end of the text you want to select, hold that left-click, and move your cursor to the other end of the text you want to select.

Another option is to use the Shift key. Go to one end of the text you want to select. Hold down the shift key and use the arrow keys to move to the other end of the text you want to select. If you arrow up or down, that will select an entire row at a time.

The text you've selected will then be highlighted in gray.

If you need to select text that isn't touching you can do this by selecting your first section of text and then holding down the Ctrl key and selecting your second section of text using your mouse. (You can't arrow to the second section of text or you'll lose your already selected text.)

Selecting an object or text box can be done with a simple left-click. Holding down the Ctrl key will let you select a second object or text box. When an object or text box is selected you will see white circles around the perimeter.

Dropdown Menu

A dropdown menu provides you a list of choices to select from. If you right-click on a PowerPoint slide, you will see an example.

Dialogue Box

Dialogue boxes are pop-up boxes that cover specialized settings. For example, when you right-click on a PowerPoint content slide and choose Font, Paragraph, or Hyperlink from the dropdown menu that will open a dialogue box.

Task Pane

Task panes are visible around the perimeter of the main workspace, but are separate. To see one, right-click on a slide and choose Format Shape from the dropdown menu. This should bring up the Format Shape task pane on the right-hand side of the main workspace.

The task pane that displays thumbnails of your presentation slides is also always visible on the left-hand side of the main workspace.

Scroll Bar

PowerPoint has multiple scroll bars that allow you to navigate through a dropdown, task pane, or your main workspace when there is more content available than is currently visible. They are located on the right-hand side and/or bottom of your workspace when needed and along the right-hand side of your task panes when needed.

Arrow

If I ever tell you to arrow to the left or right or up or down, that just means use your arrow keys.

Slider

Some options in the formatting panes on the right-hand side or in the status bar at the bottom of the PowerPoint main screen use a slider to adjust the setting. This is a horizontal line with a wider bar perpendicular to it. If you left-click on that perpendicular bar and move it to the right or the left it will adjust that particular setting upward or downward accordingly.

You can see an example of a slider in the bottom right-hand corner of PowerPoint where there is a slider to adjust the Zoom level of the main workspace.

Import From Word

It is possible to import a Word outline into PowerPoint and have PowerPoint create your slides for you using that outline. This is a very useful trick if you're someone who tends to write your presentation outline in Word first or if you're someone who is doing a mostly text-based presentation.

If you're going to do this, the first step is to create your outline in Word using Styles. (If you don't know what Styles are, I cover that in *Word 2019 Intermediate* or you can just find it using Word's help function.)

Assign the Heading 1 Style to the title you want to use for each slide. Each Heading 1 will start a new slide in your presentation.

Assign Heading 2 to your first level of bullet points, Heading 3 to the level after that, and so on.

Once you've entered all of your text into your Word document and applied the appropriate Styles, save your Word document and close it.

Next, open your PowerPoint presentation and go to the Slides section of the Home tab. Click on the dropdown arrow for New Slide and choose Slides from Outline at the bottom of the dropdown menu.

Navigate to where your Word file is saved, select it, and choose Open. PowerPoint will then use your Word outline to create a series of slides in your presentation.

Let's walk through a quick example.

Here is what I had in Word where Important Point was using the Heading 1 Style, Important Subpoint was using Heading 2, and Important Sub-Subpoint was using Heading 3:

Important Point 1

Important Point 2

Important Point 3

Important Point 4
Important Subpoint 1
Important Subpoint 2
Important Subpoint 3
Important Sub-Subpoint 1
Important Sub-Subpoint 2
Important Sub-Subpoint 3

That imported into PowerPoint as four separate slides, because I had four entries using the Heading 1 Style.

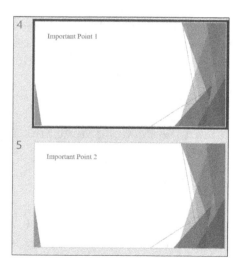
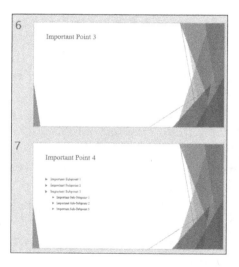

Each of the first three slides just had a title because I hadn't listed any subpoints below them.

For the fourth slide I had listed three subpoints and three sub-subpoints. Let's look more closely at that slide now:

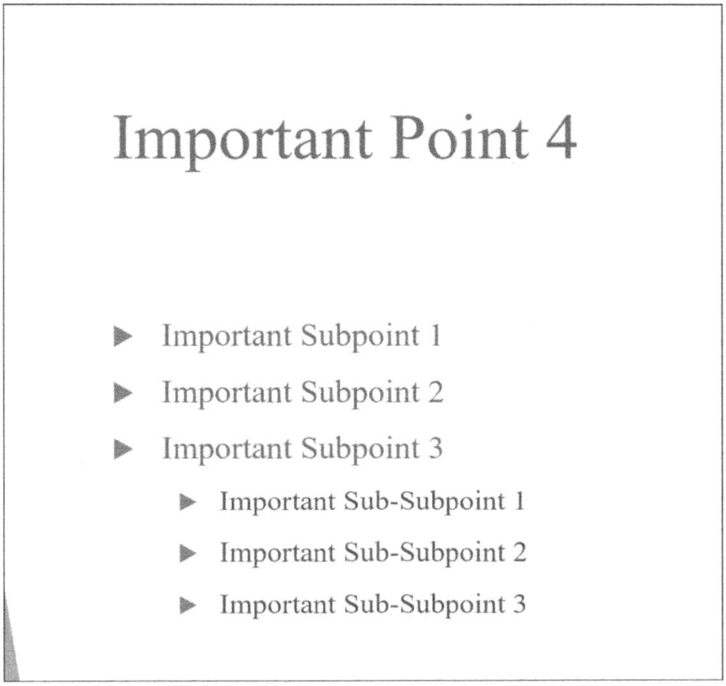

Important Point 4

▶ Important Subpoint 1

▶ Important Subpoint 2

▶ Important Subpoint 3

  ▶ Important Sub-Subpoint 1

  ▶ Important Sub-Subpoint 2

  ▶ Important Sub-Subpoint 3

You can see above that in addition to the title on this slide there are the six bulleted entries we would expect to see for the items where I applied the Heading 2 and Heading 3 style.

Although in this example I had all of my Heading 1 entries grouped together and then all of the Heading 2 entries after that and then the Headinng 3 after that, you do not have to do that.

I could have as easily used an outline that looked this this:

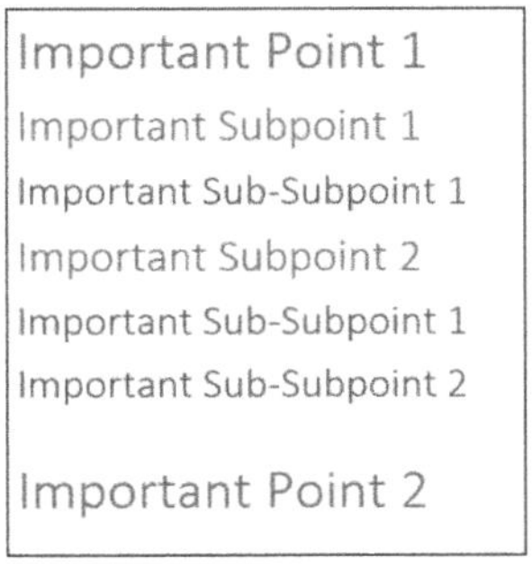

Important Point 1
Important Subpoint 1
Important Sub-Subpoint 1
Important Subpoint 2
Important Sub-Subpoint 1
Important Sub-Subpoint 2

Important Point 2

Which would have given me two presentation slides that looked like this:

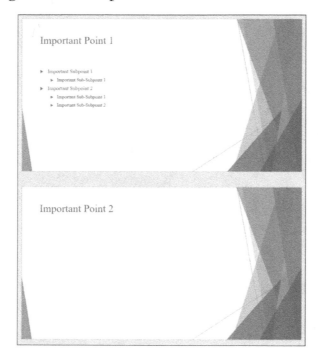

Here is a close-up of the text in the revised Slide 1:

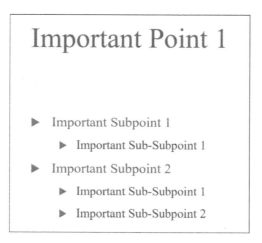

So, basically, any Outline you can put together PowerPoint can use to make your slides for you.

Additional Text and Slide Formatting Options

In *PowerPoint 2019 Beginner* we covered the majority of the text formatting options available in PowerPoint, but there were a few that were skipped. So let's cover those now.

Text Shadowing

Text shadowing is an option that allows you to add a shadow behind your text to make it stand out on the slide. To use this option, highlight the text that you want to shadow and then click on the blurry S in the bottom row of the Font section of the Home tab.

This will automatically add a shadow behind your text. You can see here an example of text that doesn't have a shadow compared to text that does:

If you want to customize the shadow attributes, right-click on a word or select more than one word and then choose Format Text Effects from the dropdown menu, and then go to the Format Shape task pane and click on the arrow next to Shadow under Text Options.

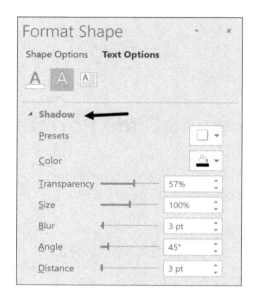

The Presets dropdown menu gives you a number of pre-defined shadowed text options. It also shows how each option would look applied to the letter A.

Or you can change the settings for Color, Transparency, Size, Blur, Angle, and Distance yourself to get a customized result.

The default is for a shadow to be a black drop shadow, but depending on the settings you choose you can add a version of the text that is substantially offset from the original text or even a blurred cloud behind the text. The best way to see your options is to play around with the settings and see what happens.

Remember that Ctrl + Z, Undo, is your friend. You can always try something and if it doesn't work use Ctrl + Z to get back to where you were before.

To remove text shadowing, use the pre-set dropdown and choose the No Shadow option.

Strikethrough

You can also format your text so that it has a strike-through, which is basically a line through the text. To add a strikethrough to your text, highlight the text, go to the Font section of the Home tab, and choose the option that has an abc with a line through it.

Another option for adding strikethrough to text is to highlight the text, right-click, choose Font from the dropdown menu, and then choose Strikethrough under the Effects section of the Font dialogue box. This approach also includes a double strikethrough option which will put two lines through the selected text.

Character Spacing

An option you may need more than strikethrough is character spacing. This one is also available through the Font section of the Home tab. It's to the right of the strikethrough option and is represented by the letters AV with a two-sided arrow below them.

What the character spacing option does is adjust the amount of space between your letters.

You have five preset options to choose from: Very Tight, Tight, Normal, Loose, and Very Loose. You can also choose More Spacing which will bring up the Font dialogue box where you can specify the exact amount to expand or condense the text.

Here is an image of the difference between the default options. That top row reads "Very Tight Spacing".

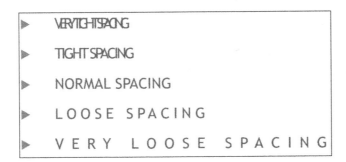

Another option for changing the character spacing is to highlight the text, right-click, choose Font from the dropdown menu, and then go to the Character Spacing tab in the Font dialogue box.

You can then choose to return the text to Normal or Expand or Condense the text using the Spacing dropdown menu. To determine the amount of spacing used, enter a value in the By box. This is the same dialogue box you'll see if you select the More Spacing option in the dropdown menu of the Font section of the Home tab.

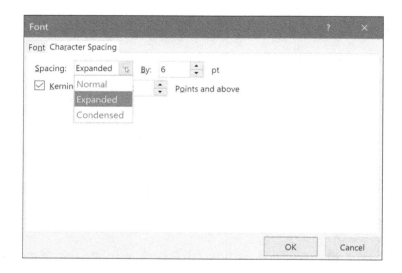

Text Direction

In *PowerPoint 2019 Beginner* we discussed how to adjust the text direction within the context of tables, but let's just go over it again here as well, because it can be used on any text in any section of a slide.

By default, at least in the U.S., text will be oriented so that it reads from left to right in a straight line.

You can change this by highlighting your text, going to the Paragraph section of the Home tab, and clicking on the dropdown arrow next to Text Direction which will give you a choice between Horizontal (which is the default), Rotate All Text 90 degrees, Rotate All Text 270 degrees, or Stacked.

(There is also a More Options choice at the bottom of the dropdown which opens a task pane, but it doesn't allow you more choices than those four. It's more useful for specifying where on the page the text will be placed.)

Your choice of text direction will impact all text in that text box. If you need to use more than one direction on a slide, you'll need multiple text boxes.

This is what the four choices look like:

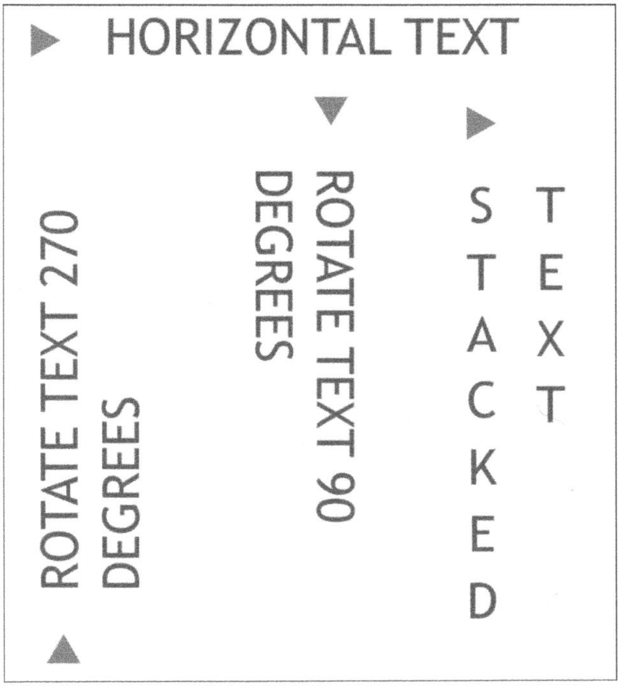

▶ HORIZONTAL TEXT

▼
ROTATE TEXT 90 DEGREES

▶
S T A C K E D
T E X T

▲
ROTATE TEXT 270 DEGREES

In order to actually have your text display in the direction you choose, you need to make sure that your text boxes are large enough to allow for that. For example, above with the Horizontal Text option I had a text box that was .44 inches tall. When I copied that and changed it to Rotate Text 270 Degrees, the text didn't rotate. I had to change the height of the text box to, in this case, be three inches before the text could properly display as rotated text.

You can also change the text direction by highlighting your text, right-clicking, choosing Format Text Effects from the dropdown menu, and then clicking on the Textbox option under Text Options (the far right-hand image) in the Format Shape task pane.

This will bring up the Text Box options. The second option is Text Direction which includes a dropdown with the four main choices available through the Home tab.

Here you can also choose to resize the text box to fit your text so that the issue I mentioned above isn't an issue.

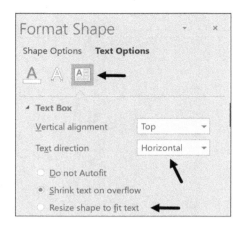

Insert a Link

It's possible to link from text in your presentation to an existing file, a web page, a place in the presentation, or to launch an email to a specific email address so that when you click on that link that item automatically opens or that task is automatically performed.

For our purposes here I'm just going to discuss linking to a web page or an existing file.

To add a link to your presentation, highlight the text that you want to turn into a link and go to the Links section of the Insert tab. From there choose the Link option.

This will bring up the Insert Hyperlink dialogue box which will then give you the option to link to an existing file or web page or another place within your presentation. You can also have the hyperlink create a new document or link to an email address.

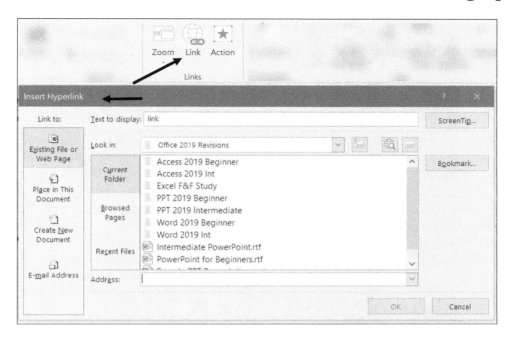

You can also open the dialogue box by selecting your text, right-clicking, and choosing Hyperlink from the dropdown menu.

The text you selected will show at the top of the dialogue box under "Text to Display". Leave this alone unless you want to amend the selected text in your presentation slide.

For linking to both files and web pages, the selection on the left, Existing File or Web Page, will already be done since that's the default.

To link to a website, add the website address at the bottom of the dialogue box where it says Address.

To link to a file use the files and folders in the middle to navigate to where the file is currently saved and click on it.

With either option you should have either a file path, file name, or a website address in the address field when you're done.

Once that's true, click on OK and PowerPoint will convert your selected text to a hyperlink.

To use the link, hold down Ctrl and click on the link. If you linked to a file it will open. If the file you wanted to link to was already opened it will take you to the beginning of the file.

If you linked to a web page, your default browser will open to that web page.

When linking files, be certain that the file will be available to open when you use the link. I have seen it happen more than once where a file was linked to a presentation but the presentation was then distributed to other users who didn't have access to the file that was linked. So, maybe it was part of a department-level shared folder that members of another department couldn't access or was on someone's laptop and so not accessible to anyone else.

This is why I generally do not recommend linking to files.

Once you have created a hyperlink, you can right-click and choose Edit Link, Copy Link, Open Link, or Remove Link from the dropdown menu. The Edit option will open a dialogue box called the Edit Hyperlink dialogue box where you can change any of the settings you want.

Copy Link will copy the link address. So, for example, for a web page you could choose to copy the link and then paste that link right into a web browser.

Open Link is another way to launch the link.

Remove Link will remove the link permanently.

Insert a Symbol

To insert a symbol, you need to click into a text box on the slide, then go to the Symbols section of the Insert tab, and click on Symbol. This will bring up the Symbol dialogue box.

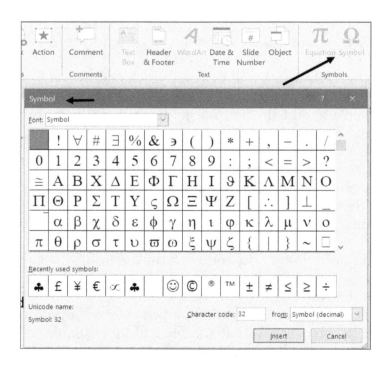

(If you're not in a text box that Symbol option will be grayed-out.)

At the bottom of the dialogue box is a listing of recently used symbols. To use one of those either double-click on it or click on it and then click on Insert. The symbol will be inserted into your slide but the dialogue box will remain open until you click on the X in the top right corner to close it.

If the recently used symbols do not contain the symbol you want, you can also use the display of symbols that takes up most of the dialogue box to find the one you want. There is a scroll bar on the right-hand side. You can also choose a specific font from the Font dropdown menu. The various Wingdings fonts are usually a good source for images.

Once a symbol has been inserted into your presentation you can change any of its attributes (color, size, spacing, etc.) just like you would any other text using the Font section of the Home tab.

Use Subscript or Superscript

On occasion you may want to use a subscript (where a portion of the text is lower than the rest, think chemical notations) or a superscript (where a portion of the text is higher than the rest, think how you would write three squared, for example).

To apply a subscript or superscript to text, highlight the text you want to raise or lower, right-click, select Font from the dropdown menu, and then choose either subscript or superscript from the Effects section of the Font dialogue box.

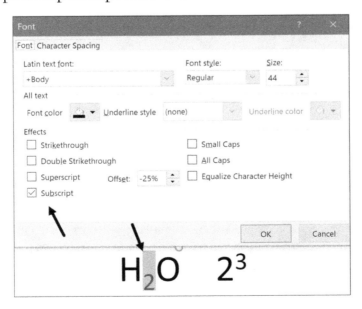

For both options you can specify the percent to which it should be offset.

(If you're writing a lot of equations there is an easier way to do subscripts and superscripts. Look to the chapter on inserting equations for a discussion.)

Format Title Section Background

If you aren't using a PowerPoint template then the slide you're working with will just have a plain white background. In general, I wouldn't recommend this unless you're putting together a presentation that you want to print and trying to save ink because an all-white slide is very generic and boring.

One option to make a slide slightly less generic is to add a fill color to the title portion of the slide. To do this, right-click in the text box for the title section and choose Format Shape from the dropdown menu. This will open a Format Shape task pane off to the right side that allows you to add a fill to that text box. Your choices are solid fill, gradient fill, picture or texture fill, pattern fill, or slide background fill.

Click on any of those options to see additional choices related to the option. For example, if I click on Solid Fill it shows me a color dropdown option as well as a transparency slider.

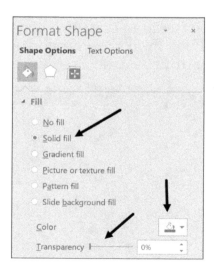

Click on the arrow next to the current color to choose from one of seventy colors. You can use the More Colors or Eyedropper options to use other colors instead.

As an example, I have pasted in an image of a book cover before and then used the Eyedropper to pull the same color used in that cover to create the background color for my slides. It's a quick and easy way to make sure the colors are consistent between a book and related presentation.

Solid Fill will do just what it says and make that text box all one color.

Gradient Fill contains pre-set options for different gradients using six basic colors which you can see in the preset gradients dropdown. If one of those works for you, just click on it.

You can also choose any color you want using the Color dropdown which is available just below the gradient stops settings.

The type, direction, angle, gradient stops, position, transparency, and brightness of a gradient can also be adjusted.

The Picture or Texture Fill option comes with a set of 24 textures to choose from (most of them hideous). If you don't like any of those choices you can use your own picture by clicking on Insert under Picture Source. There you'll have a choice to find a file, online picture, or icon. Just be sure if you use an online picture that you have the right to use that picture. Just because something is on the internet does not make it free to use.

With this option you can also customize the transparency, offset, scale, alignment, and mirror type of the image.

Pattern Fill comes with 48 patterns to choose from. The colors used with those patterns are dictated by your Foreground and Background color choices. (Here is a good time to remind you to not be overwhelming with your choices and to remember some basic color principles. Also, keep in mind that some people are color blind and that using, say red and green, will mean they can't see the pattern. Not to mention it would look ugly.)

If you're expecting to put text on top of a pattern, choose a more subtle one. (Or, better yet, go with a solid color.)

Slide background fill will apply whatever the current background on your slide is to the selected text box. (So for a generic presentation, it would make it white.)

Format Slide Background

In the same way that you can add a background to a text box like the title section of a slide, you can do so to the entire background of a slide.

To do this, go to the Customize section of the Design tab and click on Format Background. This will open the Format Background task pane.

You can also right-click on the outer edge of a slide (outside of a text box) and choose Format Background from the dropdown menu which will also open the same task pane.

From there you can choose between solid fill, gradient fill, picture or texture fill, and pattern fill just like you could with a text box.

I will add the same cautions here as I did above that you need to be careful with a background fill that you don't overwhelm the presentation and make it unreadable. You have more leeway here because your text boxes will be a solid color and sit on top of whatever pattern you choose, but still. Don't distract from the words.

Here's an example where I've applied a background pattern and then used solid colors for the two main text boxes and made sure that the font color for each of those text boxes contrasted enough with the background to be visible.

I went with one of the more subtle background patterns but this still may be a little too busy for the average user. If you really want to be that creative, I'd encourage you to explore the provided PowerPoint templates before you try to create your own background and color scheme.

But if you want to do it yourself, that's how. The possibilities are endless. Which is a good thing when you need that and a very bad thing when you're not capable of editing yourself. Like this example:

For those of you reading in print, the color version is much much worse but even in black and white the gradients, transparency, and patterns are not helping. Remember, the presentation is there to help you convey information. If it distracts from your message so much that no one hears what you say, then you've failed.

Equations

If you're working with mathematical symbols or equations, PowerPoint actually comes with certain common equations that you can just insert into your presentation without worrying about how to find all the appropriate symbols to create them.

To use these equations, go to the Symbols section of the Insert tab, and click on the dropdown arrow under Equation.

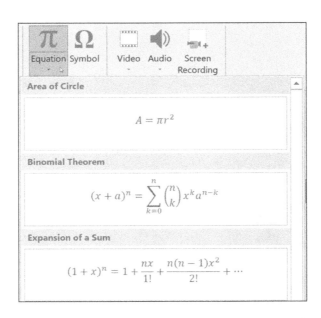

The equations that are available pre-formatted are the area of a circle, the binomial theorem, the expansion of a sum, the Fourier series, the Pythagorean theorem, the quadratic formula, the Taylor expansion, and two trig identities, one involving the sum or subtraction of the sine of two values and one involving the sum of the cosine of two values.

To insert one of these equations into your presentation slide, click on it.

For a blank slide, the equation will insert into the slide in a text box. If you were already clicked into a text box on an existing slide, it will insert as text at the point where your cursor was.

Once you insert an equation into your presentation, an Equation Tools Design tab will also appear. It lets you build any equation you could possibly want and includes common symbols and structures that are used in equations.

Here is the Structures section of that tab:

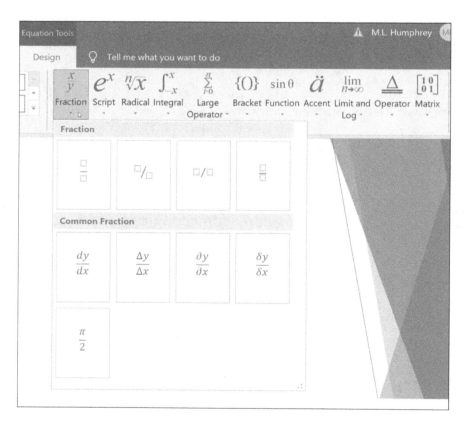

To insert a structure or symbol, simply click on it and the symbol or structure will be inserted at the point where your cursor was in the text box on that slide.

Some of the structures you insert will have dotted squares, like you can see in the Fraction section above. These allow for additional inputs. Click one of the squares and you can then add another structure or type in numbers.

Another way to bring up the Equation Tools Design tab is to go to the Equations dropdown in the Symbols section of the Insert tab and choose Insert New Equation from the bottom of the dropdown menu. That will bring up the tab and you will see text in your slide that says "Type equation here."

If you have a stylus or are just very good at writing with your mouse (I certainly am not), you can also choose the Ink Equation option. This will pop-up a dialogue box where you can "write" the equation and PowerPoint will convert it into typed text. I was able to get it to do 2+3 for me. Without a stylus I'm not sure I could write a big calculus formula, though. But it is an option.

Okay.

For each equation there are three display options available in the Tools section on the left-hand side of the Equation Tools Design tab: professional, linear, and normal. Here is an example of the area of a circle equation written in each format:

▶ Professional: $A = \pi r^2$

▶ Linear: $A = \pi r^\wedge 2$

▶ Normal: $A=\pi r^2$

To edit an existing equation, click anywhere within the equation to make the Equation Tools Design tab available and then choose your preferred format.

You can also change the size of the text in your equation by selecting the text and then using the Font section of the Home tab like you would with any other text. If the text is formatted as Professional you can't change the font from Cambria Math, but you can still change the font size and add bolding, italics, etc.

WordArt

Now we come to WordArt, which for a normal corporate presentation is probably not a good idea. Remember the whole adage about not letting the presentation get in the way of what you're presenting.

But there will be people who want to use it. And there may be settings in which it makes sense to do so. (I know a few people who, for example, design book covers in PowerPoint.)

So. Let's cover it.

What WordArt does is inserts text into your presentation that has various enhancements added such as a fill color, border color, and/or shading. Or, sometimes, all three. Like here:

Your text here

You can insert WordArt by going to the Text section of the Insert tab and choosing from the WordArt dropdown menu.

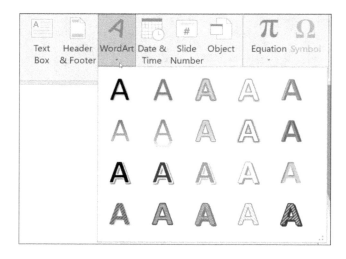

Initially you'll have twenty choices of format to choose from. Click on one of those choices and PowerPoint will insert a text box with that formatting that includes the words "Your text here". You can then replace that text with your own and it will keep the formatting you chose.

Another way to get to the same formatting options is to type text into a slide and then use the Drawing Tools Format tab, which should be visible as long as you're clicked onto your text. It has a WordArt Styles section that includes those twenty pre-formatted options as well as dropdowns for Text Fill, Text Outline, and Text Effects.

By making selections from the Text Fill, Text Outline, and Text Effects dropdowns in the WordArt Styles section of the Drawing Tools Format tab you can create a completely customized style for your text.

If you click on the expansion arrow for the WordArt Styles section that will open the Format Shape task pane. For me it defaulted to a section that had the Text Effects options. The Text Fill and Text Outline options were in a separate section to the left of the Text Effects. You can also open that pane by right-clicking on your text and choosing Format Text Effects from the dropdown menu.

So, what are your options?

Text Fill allows you to change the surface of the letters to be any solid color, a gradient, or a texture. You can also use a photo for the surface of your text.

If you want to use a gradient that is a specific color, so let's say shaded green text, you need to choose the color first and then the gradient option because otherwise choosing the color will convert it back to a solid color.

I kind of find their texture options hideous, but the picture option would allow you to bring in any texture you'd like to use on your letters. (Or you can in fact use a real picture. I've seen that done on book covers.)

The Text Outline option allows you to add or change the color, weight, and style of the line used along the border of each letter. If you use the task pane there are options for transparency (which will make the border appear lighter in color than your selected color choice) and additional line types.

The Text Effects option allows you to apply a shadow, a reflection, a glow, a bevel, a 3-D rotation, or a transformation to your text. Transformations place text along a path or "warp" the text into various shapes. You can see the options in the secondary dropdown menu.

If you use the curved text effect, you will likely need to adjust the size of the text box to get the text to curve the way you want it to. You may also need to force text onto different lines or add extra spaces if trying to create a circle of text like this one:

So a lot you can do with WordArt. It's fantastic for things like creating a logo or some other artistic imagery. But it should still be used with caution for a basic professional presentation.

Alright. Now let's talk about shapes.

Shapes

Insert Shapes

You can also insert a wide variety of shapes into your presentation. This can be done via the Drawing section of the Home tab, the Insert Shapes section of the Drawing Tools Format tab, or the Illustrations section of the Insert tab (under the Shapes dropdown). Here is what the option looks like in the Home tab:

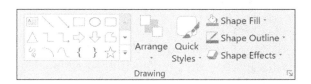

If you click on the down-pointing arrow with a line above it, you'll see a much larger set of shapes to choose from. They fall into the categories of Recently Used Shapes, Lines, Rectangles, Basic Shapes, Block Arrows, Equation Shapes, Flowchart, Stars and Banners, Callouts, and Action Buttons.

The most common shape I insert is the first one shown, which is a text box. It's the A in the corner of a box with lines in it.

To insert a text box into your presentation slide, click on the text box option and then click onto your presentation slide. The inserted shape will be equivalent to one character. You can then type text and it will expand in size as you type.

You can also left-click and drag to the side and up or down to create a text box before you start typing. This can be especially useful when you're not yet ready to add text, but do want to define the space in which you plan to add text.

The same process works for other objects as well. So if I want to insert a downward pointing arrow, I just select that option from my menu and then either click onto my presentation slide or click and drag to get the size I want.

If you have issues inserting a text box or other shape into your presentation slide, try inserting it in an area that doesn't already have a text box in it and then dragging the text box to where you want it to go.

Some shapes may require multiple clicks to create or may require that you left-click and hold as you move your cursor around to draw them.

For example:

Scribble requires a left-click and hold as you then scribble on your slide.

Freeform: Shape will close and complete once you connect your last point to your beginning point, You can either click and hold as you create a scribbled shape that connects back to the starting point or you can click multiple times to create a series of straight lines that are only complete when you click back on the origin.

Curve will anchor and curve your line from the anchor point each time you click on the presentation. You'll see the curve when you move your mouse away from each anchor point. It will only stop making new curves when you use Esc or Enter or connect back to the origin.

Change Shape Size

To change the size of an inserted shape or object, you have a few options. If you click on it you'll see white circles around the perimeter. You can click and drag on one of those white circles to change the height or width of the object. If you want to do so proportionately, click on one of the circles in the corner and drag at an angle.

You can also use the Size section of the Drawing Tools Format tab. By default it will change height and width separate from one another so skew your shape.

A better option if keeping the shape's proportions the same matters, is to right-click and choose Format Shape from the dropdown menu.

This will open the Format Shape task pane. Click on the Size & Properties choice under Shape Options and then expand the Size dropdown. The checkbox there for Lock Aspect Ratio will ensure that when you adjust the height the width also adjusts or vice versa.

You can then adjust the height or the width value and know that the other value will adjust as well to keep the image the shape the same as you increase or decrease its size.

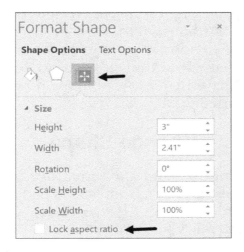

Adjust Shape Form

For shapes that consist of multiple curves or lines, you can also adjust the individual segments.

For some shapes, like arrows, you will have one or more yellow circles that appear when you click on the shape. You can click on that yellow circle and drag to change the location of the anchor point. For arrows this lets you make the base of the arrow wider or narrower or change where the point of the arrow begins.

For other shapes, like Scribble, you can instead right-click and choose Edit Points from the dropdown. This will place a number of black boxes along the outline of the shape. You can then click on any of those boxes and drag them to alter the shape.

Edit Points is also available in the Insert Shapes section of the Drawing Tools Format tab under Edit Shape.

For a line with an arrow at the end, you can change the direction the arrow is pointing by clicking and dragging the white circle at the pointed end.

For a two-dimensional arrow you can change the direction of the arrow along a straight line that way (so left to right, top to bottom), but to rotate it to the side you'd need to use the rotation option that appears along the edge of the shape. (An arrow that forms a circle pointing to the right. Click on it and drag.)

You can also flip horizontal or vertical or rotate 90 degrees using the Rotate option in the Arrange section of the Drawing Tools Format tab.

Choose More Rotation Options from the bottom of that dropdown to open the Format Shape task pane where you can change the rotation to any degrees between -3600 and 3600. (Although 0 to 360 is actually all you need).

Note that the degree of rotation is based upon the starting point of the shape. So if you had an arrow that was already pointed off to the right then a rotation of ninety degrees would have that arrow pointing downward since that's ninety degrees from where it started.

Change Shape

You can change an existing shape to a different one by clicking on it and then going to the Drawing Tools Format tab and choosing Edit Shape from the Insert Shapes section and then choosing Change Shape which will show you all available shapes. Select the one you want.

Fill, Outline, and Effects

Just like with WordArt, you can change the fill, outline, and effects for a shape. First, click on the shape you want to change and then go to the Drawing Tools Format tab.

There are a number of pre-formatted Shape Styles that you can choose from in the Shape Styles section.

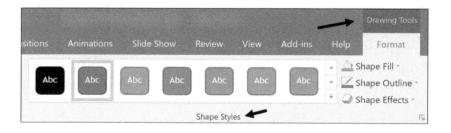

The colors used there will be colors that match your chosen theme. Hold your mouse over each one to see it applied to your shape. Click on it to permanently apply it.

You can also find these options under the Quick Styles dropdown in the Drawing section of the Home tab.

If you want more control over the appearance of your shape, you can use the Shape Fill, Shape Outline, or Shape Effects options available in those same sections.

The Shape Fill, Shape Outline, and Shape Effect options work the exact same way as the Text Fill, Text Outline, and Text Effects options did with WordArt. Your default color choices will be related to the theme colors. You can click on More Colors to choose any colors you want.

Just, you know, remember your audience and don't get too carried away.

Move Shapes Relative to One Another

If you have more than one shape in a presentation slide then you're probably going to end up wanting to move those shapes around relative to one another.

This is done using the Arrange options which are available either in the Drawing section of the Home tab or in the Arrange section of the Drawing Tools Format tab.

The Align object options are located in the secondary dropdown menu in the Position Objects section.

You can also just right-click on shapes to bring them forward/back or to group them once you've selected more than one.

Bring Forward/Send Backward

To change the order of overlapping objects, use bring to front, send to back, bring forward, and send backward options.

When dealing with bringing shapes forward or moving them backward, think of the shapes as stacked one on top of the other with the "top" of the stack in the front. This is the layer that will be fully visible. If that shape overlaps another shape then where the two overlap you will only see the topmost shape. Any portion of the other shape will be hidden.

You can either move a shape one level at a time (with bring forward or send backward) or all the way to the front or back at once (with bring to front or send to back).

You might use this, for example, if you had a triangle and a text box on a slide and wanted to put the text box on top of the triangle. To make this work, you might need to tell PowerPoint to move the text box forward so that it was visible on top of the triangle or to move the triangle backward so that it was behind the text box.

Group Objects

To group or ungroup objects use the Group, Ungroup, and Regroup options.

Group takes multiple shapes that you've selected and lets you move them around or resize them as one unit. So, for example, with that text box and triangle combination, I'd want to group those two elements once I had them properly aligned to one another so that if I had to resize or move them I wouldn't lose that work.

Align Objects

And then there's a whole set of options for positioning objects that lets you align those objects to one another or to various portions of the presentation slide.

The alignment options are align left, center, right, top, middle, or bottom as well as distribute horizontally, distribute vertically, and align to slide.

Whichever alignment choice you make will only include the shapes you select. The other shapes on the slide will not move.

If you choose the option at the bottom of the dropdown to Align Selected Objects, then the selected objects will align relative to one another.

If you choose to Align To Slide instead, then the slide will basically be treated as another shape and your shapes will align to it.

Which direction your shapes move to align will depend on their position relative to one another and the alignment choice you make. So align left will move all shapes to align along the left-most edge of the left-most shape. Align right will move all shapes to align along the right-most edge of the right-most shape. Align middle will move all selected shapes to align along the midline between the left-most edge and the right-most edge of those shapes.

Here is an illustration of the six alignment choices using two equally-sized but offset arrows to demonstrate. The middle, lighter-colored, row of arrows shows the original position of the arrows. The top row has the results of applying Left, Center, and Right to those arrows. The bottom row has the result of applying Top, Middle, and Bottom.

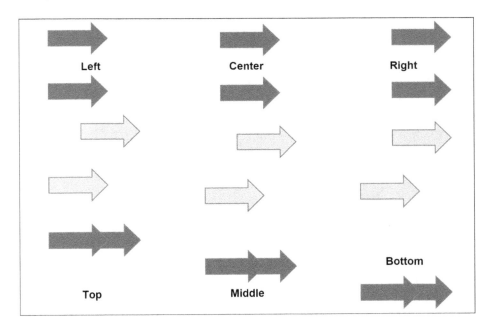

In the top row the arrows have moved horizontally. For Left you can see that both arrows moved so that they were aligned along the left-most side of their combined space. For Center they both aligned along the center point of their combined space. For Right they aligned along the rightmost edge of their combined space.

On the bottom row the arrows have moved vertically. For Top they aligned along the topmost edge off their combined space. For Middle they aligned along the midline of their combined space. And for Bottom they aligned along the bottom edge.

Distribute Horizontally will distribute the selected objects equidistant along a horizontal line within their combined space. Distribute Vertically will do so along a vertical line.

These were objects aligned to one another. If I'd instead aligned them to the slide then they would have been moved relative to the area of the slide or the active workspace of the slide.

Selection Pane

If you have a large number of shapes on a presentation slide, you can use the Selection Pane which is available in the Arrange section of the Drawing Tools Format tab. Clicking on this option will open a new task pane on the right-hand side of the screen that shows every single shape on that slide. You can then select any of the shapes that you want to group or align from that pane rather than trying to select them on the presentation slide itself, although the names PowerPoint assigns each object may not be all that helpful.

To close this pane just click on the x in the top corner.

(If you ever need to select all of the objects on a presentation slide at once, Ctrl + A also works. Just be sure to click outside of any text boxes before doing so or it will just select all of the text in the text box instead of the objects on the slide.)

Action Buttons

There is a special type of shape that you can insert into a presentation that's called an action button. They're available in the very last section of the shapes dropdown menu.

To see what each one does, hold your mouse over it. For example, the first item in that list is described as "Action Button: Go Back or Previous".

Once you insert an action button you can click on that button to perform the specified action.

Unlike the other shapes, when you insert an action button into your presentation this will open a dialogue box where you then need to provide additional information so that the action represented by the shape can be performed.

There is a dropdown menu available in the Action Settings dialogue box that allows you to choose different actions than just the default. You can set an action button to take you pretty much anywhere in your presentation or another presentation or a URL address or even open a file.

The dialogue box that you'll see for each action button is the same one but the default settings will be different depending on the action button you selected.

For example, the sound action button has by default the play sound option checked and an applause sound file selected. (Again there is a dropdown menu provided with numerous sounds to choose from including a custom sound file.)

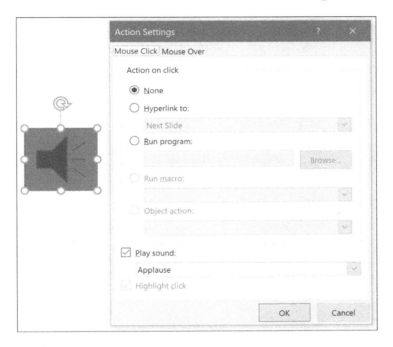

You can either set an action to occur when you click on it or when you move your mouse over it. The default is for the action to occur when you click on the action button.

To change the settings for an action button you've already placed in your presentation, right-click on the action button image and choose the Edit Link option from the dropdown menu or click onto the action button and then choose Link from the Links section of the Insert tab.

Also, the appearance of an action button can be modified the same way any other shape can be modified so you don't have to stick to the default shape that PowerPoint uses for that action.

Rulers, Gridlines, and Guides

Okay, now let's talk about a few tools that will assist you in positioning your elements on a presentation slide visually instead of by using the alignment options. Namely, rulers, gridlines, and guidelines.

If you go to the Show section of the View tab you'll see that there are three options listed on the left-hand side: ruler, gridlines, and guides. If the boxes are checked, they're in use, if they're not checked they're not in use.

You can also right-click outside of a content box on any presentation slide to see options for Grid and Guides and for Ruler in the dropdown menu.

When gridlines are turned on you should be able to see very subtle dotted lines in the background that intersect to form equally-sized squares across the entire presentation slide except at the edges where the squares are only partial squares. Each complete square is one inch by one inch.

These lines are not visible during a presentation or when the presentation is printed, but when I'm dragging items around on a presentation slide. I will often align the items along these gridlines.

Guides are lines that run across the slide at any point you specify. They can be either horizontal or vertical. To add one, right-click on your presentation slide, go to Grid and Guides, and then choose Add Vertical Guide or Add Horizontal Guide. The guide will initially be placed in the exact center of the slide and will be a dotted line that goes off the edge of the slide.

To move a guideline, hover your mouse over it until you see two parallel lines with arrows pointing out from them, then left-click and drag. As you drag the guideline you should see a number. This number indicates how far the line is from the center point of the presentation. The directional arrow next to the number indicates the direction from the center point.

So a right arrow next to a 1.25 means that the guideline is 1.25 inches to the right of the center of the slide.

Guidelines are also not visible during a presentation or on a printed slide. They are just meant to help you place the elements in your presentation.

The Ruler option will add a ruler along the left-hand side and top of the presentation. The ruler is numbered from the center point of the slide. So you can see that it will go from say 6.5 to 6.5 with a mid-point of zero.

Rather than adjust the size of a shape in the Drawing Tools Format tab by specifying a value, I will often just click and drag and use the gridlines, guidelines, or ruler to determine where to stop.

Headers and Footers

You can add headers or footers to your slides or handouts fairly easily. For slides you can only add a footer, for handouts it's a header and/or a footer.

To do so, go to the Text section of the Insert tab and click on Header & Footer. This will bring up the Header and Footer dialogue box.

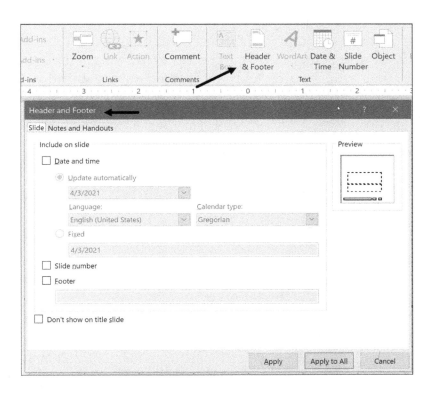

You can also reach the Header and Footer dialogue box by clicking on either the Date & Time or Slide Number options in the Text section of the Insert tab.

There are two tabs available in the dialogue box, one for your slide and the other for notes and handouts.

You can add three different items to the footer of a slide: date and time, slide number, and/or custom text (under the Footer heading).

For date and time, click on the box next to where it says Date and Time. Be very careful here if you choose to update automatically because that may not be what you actually intended. If you make that choice then every single time the document is opened the date and time will change. This is a mistake I often see made with memo fields where people use automatic date and time and then forget they've done so and the date on the memo keeps changing every time someone opens it.

The other option is to choose a fixed date and input the date you want.

You can include the slide number at the bottom of a slide by clicking on the checkbox next to Slide Number.

You can also insert customized text in the footer by checking the box next to Footer and then typing in whatever text you want.

The final item on the slide tab indicates whether you want those items included on your title slide. I usually do not.

You can see where each item in the footer will be placed in the preview on the right-hand side of the dialogue box. This varies by template. For the template I'm currently using, the Footer text was placed in the bottom left, the date towards the bottom right, and the slide number a little further to the right. When I switched it to a different template the date went in the left, the text went to the right, and the slide number stayed on the far right.

(You can adjust these placements by editing the Master Slides for the template, which we'll discuss later. Just be careful if you do that. It can go wrong fast.)

Finally, you can either apply your footer to that specific slide by choosing Apply or to all slides in your deck by choosing Apply To All. Usually you'll want to apply to all.

To add a header or footer to your notes and handouts, click on the Notes and Handouts tab in the dialogue box instead. You can then add the date and time, a page number, a customized header, or a customized footer to your notes and handouts.

Remember, this is not for the presentation itself, but rather for the notes or handouts that can be generated related to the presentation.

Once more, the preview off to the side will show you where each element will appear on the document. As you click on an item its location will be outlined with a darker border. But you need to pay attention to see which one it is because if you have more than one item checked there will be more than one location outlined with a darker border. You can check and uncheck the boxes to see the location for each item if you really need to.

Charts

Now let's talk about how to insert a chart into a presentation.

Insert a Chart

To insert a chart, you can bring up a content-type slide and then click on the second image on the top row which looks like a column chart with three columns. If you hold your mouse over the icon it will say Insert Chart.

You can also go to the Illustrations section of the Insert tab and choose Chart from there.

Whichever you choose, this will bring up the Insert Chart dialogue box.

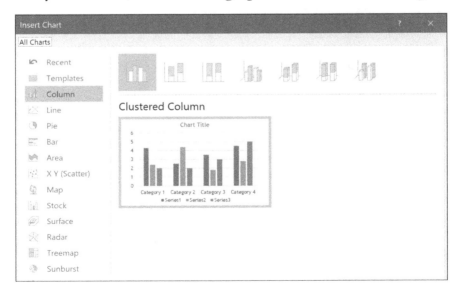

(If you're familiar with Microsoft Excel, you'll notice that this is almost identical to the dialogue box that you see in Excel when you choose to insert a chart.)

The main chart types are displayed along the left-hand side and the sub-types of those charts are along the top. Click on any chart to see a sample displayed in the main area of the dialogue box.

By default, when a chart is inserted into your presentation the colors will match your chosen theme.

To insert a chart into your presentation, click on the chart type you want, and then click on OK in the bottom right corner of the dialogue box.

So, for example, if I want an X Y scatter chart with markers, I'd click on X Y (Scatter) on the left-hand side and then click on the second or fourth option up top depending on whether I wanted my data points connected with a curved or a straight line.

Once you click on OK, PowerPoint will insert that chart type into your slide and show you a pre-populated data table in a spreadsheet window that uses dummy data. Replace that data with your own and you will have a completed chart.

For me just now the spreadsheet window was too small to show the data, so I had to move my cursor to the lower edge of the window until I could see a two-sided arrow and then I left-clicked and expanded that window until I could actually see the data.

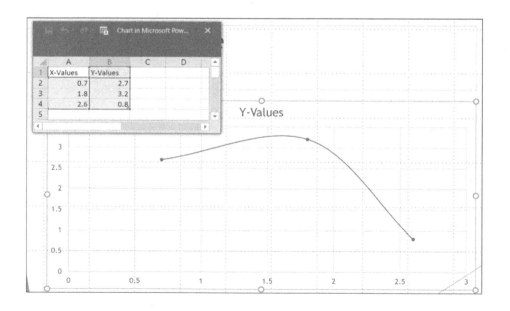

We'll return to how to change that data later, but first I want to discuss the different chart types you have to choose from.

For those of you who have already read *Excel 2019 Intermediate* or *Excel 2019 Charts* you can skip this section because it's going to be the same. For those who aren't familiar with the different types of charts, read on.

Note that I am only covering here the most common chart types: column, bar, line, pie, doughnut, and scatter.

Chart Types

Column Charts

The first chart option listed is Column. There are seven possible column charts that you can choose from, but I'm going to focus on the first three choices, which are the 2-D versions, since most of the 3-D versions are the same except three-dimensional.

For 2-D, you can choose from clustered columns, stacked columns, and 100% stacked columns. Here is an example of all three using the exact same data:

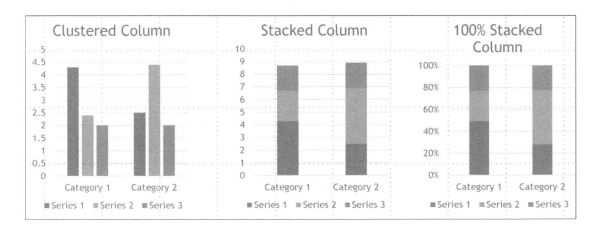

The difference between the clustered columns and the stacked columns is that the clustered columns version puts the results for each series side-by-side for each category.

You can easily see the height difference between different results, but it can quickly become too busy if you're dealing with a large number of entries.

For example, I have nine sales channels I track across months. Having nine columns side-by-side for each of twelve months would be overwhelming.

(I'm using series and category here even though those aren't the most comfortable terms for me because that's what PowerPoint uses as the defaults when it builds a chart. For me, Category is generally a time period and Series is generally one of my vendors or one of my titles. So I'll do a column chart of sales per title per month or sales per vendor per month. Just wanted to mention that in case it helps you as well since I don't think most people think in terms of series across categories. Anyway.)

For me the stacked columns option is a better choice than the clustered columns choice. Like with clustered columns, stacked columns have different column heights for each series based on their value, but the columns are stacked one atop the other for each category instead of shown side-by-side which means you end up with only one column per category.

The stacked columns option lets you see the overall change from time period to time period based on the total height of the column as well as for each variable based upon its absolute size as part of that column.

The final option, the 100% stacked columns option, presents all of the information in one column just like stacked columns does. But instead of basing each section's height on its value, it shows the percentage share of the whole.

While you lose any measurement of value (a column chart with values of 2:5:5 will look the exact same as one with values of 20:50:50 or 200:500:500), you can better see changes in percentage share for a given series. (A variable that goes from 10% share to 50% share will be clearly visible.)

As mentioned above, the first three 3-D column chart options are the same as the 2-D options. The only difference is that the bars are three-dimensional instead of two-dimensional. This can sometimes make a chart in a PowerPoint presentation more dynamic, but it can also come off as gimmicky, so use it with caution. My preference is to use charts that keep the focus on the data and not my fancy schmancy presentation skills.

The final 3-D option is a more advanced chart type that creates a three-variable graph. I'm not going to cover that in further detail here since it's more of an advanced topic, but know that it is available for those who want it.

Line Charts

Line charts are the next chart type. There are again seven options listed, but I would recommend if you're not sure what you're doing to only use the first and the fourth options, which are line and line with markers.

These are the standard line graph most of us are used to where the line height corresponds to the values of what's being charted.

The other options are line graph equivalents of the stacked and 100% stacked column graphs. In 2020 I did see a fair number of these actually used for charting outcomes by age group where there was a line for each age group and the height of the top-most line was the overall occurrence.

However, each time I saw those used I also saw that the area under each line was filled in with color so that it was not just plain lines on the chart. I'd still strongly recommend against using the stacked and 100% stacked options as plain lines. If you do use them, fill in the space below the lines to make it clear that the lines are not absolute values.

The 3-D line chart option is a more advanced chart type that creates an actual three-variable line graph and we're not going to cover that here. You can use it to create a two-variable line graph with a three-dimensional line, but don't. Keep it simple.

Here are examples of the basic line chart and the line chart with markers:

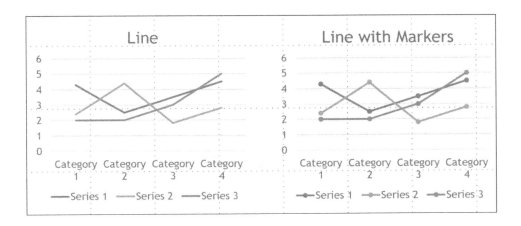

Pie and Doughnut Charts

Next we have pie and doughnut charts, which are both listed under the heading of pie charts.

Pie and doughnut charts are best used when are looking at only one series per category. So, for example, I use them for annual results by title or by vendor. The sample charts PowerPoint provides show quarterly results.

There are three two-dimensional pie chart options, one three-dimensional pie chart option, and one doughnut chart option.

The three-dimensional pie chart option is the same as the basic pie chart except in three-dimensions. The doughnut chart is basically a hollowed out version of a basic pie chart.

Here are examples of the three two-dimensional pie chart options:

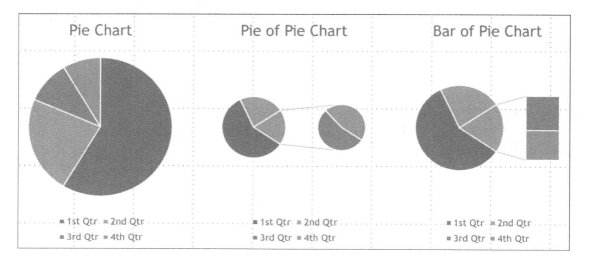

You can choose between a standard pie chart, a pie of pie chart, or a bar of pie chart

If you're only focused on who or what accounts for the biggest share, then you should just use the standard pie chart or the doughnut chart.

If you want to be able to clearly see the results for all of your segments, even the smallest ones, then the pie of pie chart or the bar of pie chart are potentially better choices.

The pie of pie chart creates one main pie chart in which it combines a number of the smaller results to form one segment of the chart. It then breaks out those smaller results into their own pie chart where they each take up their proportion of that smaller part of the pie.

So, for example, in the sample we're seeing here, 3rd quarter and 4th quarter were combined in the left-hand pie chart. 1st quarter is 58%, 2nd quarter is 23%, and then 3rd and 4th quarter combined are 19%. In the second pie chart you have 3rd and 4th quarter. 3rd quarter is only 10% of all four quarters, but 53% of the combination of the 3rd and 4th quarter values so in the second pie chart it shows as a little more than half of that pie chart.

Personally, I find it visually confusing. You can adjust the size of the secondary pie chart to help with that issue, but it's still something that I have to stop and think about.

The bar of pie chart does something similar except it creates a bar chart with the smaller values instead of a pie chart.

In order to avoid confusion, the bar of pie chart is probably the better choice of the two, but honestly I wouldn't use either one if you can avoid it. (The best charts can be read without explanation and I'm not sure that would be true for either of these for your average user. Maybe for a specialized audience where these types of charts are used often, but be wary.)

Also, if the secondary chart doesn't include the results you think it should, sort your data table from largest to smallest and see if that fixes the issue.

Bar Charts

Your next option is a bar chart. Bar charts are just like column charts, except on their side, with a clustered, stacked, and 100% stacked option available in both two-dimensional and three-dimensional versions.

Scatter Charts

The final chart type I'm going to cover here is the X Y or scatter chart (or plot).

Scatter charts plot the value of variable A given a value for variable B. There are five scatter plot options as well as two bubble plot options. We're not going to discuss the bubble plot options here.

The first scatter plot option is the classic scatter plot. It takes variable A and plots it against variable B, creating a standalone data point for each observation. It doesn't care what order your entries are in, because there's no attempt to connect those entries to form a pattern.

The other four scatter plot options include lines drawn through each plotted point. The two smooth line options try to draw the best curved line between points. The straight line options just connect point 1 to point 2 to point 3 using straight lines between each point. The charts with markers show each of the data points on the line, the charts without markers do not.

PowerPoint draws the line from the first set of coordinates you provide to the second to the third, etc. This introduces a time component into your data since the order you list the data points in impacts the appearance of the line. If you have data where the order of the measurements doesn't matter and you still want to draw a line through the points, then you'll want to sort your data by one of the variables before you create your scatter plot.

Here is an example of a basic scatter plot, one with straight lines, and one with smooth lines that uses markers:

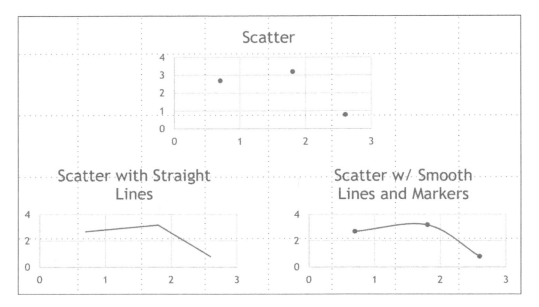

You can also use scatter plots to chart more than one set of results. You just need to add another column to the provided data table so you can input the values for the second set of results. (The spreadsheet provided by PowerPoint is going to work just like it would in Excel. The only difference is that PowerPoint gives you a data table to start with whereas Excel does not.)

Entering Data via PowerPoint

I would highly recommend that if you're going to work with charts in PowerPoint that you become familiar with working with them in Excel. Because basically that's what you're doing. The chart you create just happens to be displayed in PowerPoint.

When you insert a chart into PowerPoint it gives you a data table with pre-filled values. You can simply type over those values by clicking into the cells in the provided spreadsheet and replacing them with your values. Another option is to copy and paste your data from Excel into the data table provided by PowerPoint.

For me the data table often opened as too small a window to actually see the data. If that happens to you, just increase the size of the Excel window until you can see everything.

You can also paste in more data than is in the sample. For example, I took the pie chart that by default has four values and pasted in seven values just fine.

(The chart will update immediately. If it updates fine but you can't see your new data in the Excel window, check your formatting for those cells.)

If you already inserted the table and now need to edit the data for that table, either right-click on the chart and choose Edit Data from the dropdown menu or click on the chart and then go to the Data section of the Chart Tools Design tab and click on the dropdown for Edit Data there.

Your choices are to Edit Data or Edit Data in Excel. For me both options open a small Excel window with a name of Chart in Microsoft PowerPoint.

The data that's already being used in the chart will be shown, just overwrite or edit that. If you need to add more data than is currently being used, do so in the same columns as the existing data.

Importing An External Chart

Another option is to just do everything in Excel and then copy and paste the chart you created in Excel into your PowerPoint slide. I just did that and the chart even pasted into PowerPoint using my theme colors.

I was also able to change the colors, fonts, etc. of the pasted chart once it was in PowerPoint. But be careful because when I tried to Refresh my data it erased all my values.

When you paste from Excel instead of designing your chart in PowerPoint, the data behind the chart is still in that Excel spreadsheet, not PowerPoint. So when you choose to Edit Data, you will be editing data in your source worksheet. (Which means there's a potential to break your presentation if that file is no longer available.)

It's not the best option, really, but very quick and easy for those of us who are more comfortable in Excel than PowerPoint. I'd probably only use it for charts I know are done and ready to go and then I'd paste them in as Pictures that can't be edited at all. But at least they wouldn't break if I moved or renamed the source file. And no one would be able to refresh them and erase all their data.

Change Chart Type

To change your chart type, right-click on the chart and choose Change Chart Type from the dropdown menu.

You can also click on the chart and then click on Change Chart Type in the Type section of the Chart Tools Design tab.

Either way this will open the Change Chart Type dialogue box where you can select your new chart type and then click on OK to apply the change.

Keep in mind when changing chart types that certain chart types, like column and bar charts, are easily interchangeable, but other chart types, like line and pie charts, are not.

Chart Styles

To quickly format a chart, you can choose from the Chart Styles section of the Chart Tools Design tab. This section has various layout options for each chart type that include different fills, backgrounds, labels, etc.

You can hold your mouse over each one to see it applied to your chart. Click on an option to keep it.

I personally tend not to like most of the choices, but it can be a good way to get close to what you want and then you can edit to a final layout from there.

Quick Layout

There is also a Quick Layout dropdown menu in the Chart Layouts section of the Chart Tools Design tab. These quick layouts generally involve different label arrangements and data displays. If you hold your mouse over each one you'll see it applied to your chart and also see a description of what attributes are included in that layout.

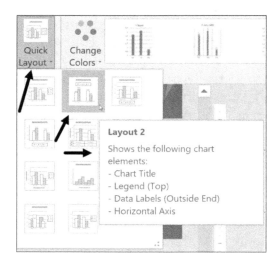

You can apply both a Chart Style and a Quick Layout to a chart, but the order in which you do so may impact the appearance and which attributes are kept and which are overwritten. I just took two identical charts and applied the same Chart

Style and Quick Layout to both of them but in different orders. The results were similar but one ended up with narrower columns, the legends on the two charts were in different locations, and one of the two had major gridlines while the other didn't. All because of the order in which I applied the two choices.

Change Colors

If you just want to mix up the colors in your chart, there are a number of pre-formatted options available under the Change Colors option in the Chart Styles section of the Chart Tools Design tab.

If you're working with one of the PowerPoint templates, the list of choices will use your theme colors. You can choose Colorful (multiple colors) or Monochromatic (different shades of one color) options.

Chart Elements

Charts come with a variety of optional elements that you can add, edit, or remove. This includes axes, axis titles, chart titles, data labels, data tables, error bars, gridlines, legends, series lines, trendlines, or up/down bars. Which ones are available depends on the chart type.

To edit your chart elements, go to the Add Chart Element dropdown menu in the Chart Layouts section of the Chart Tools Design tab. (On the far left.)

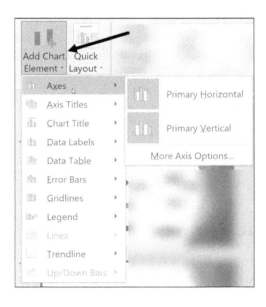

Elements that aren't available will be grayed out like Lines and Up/Down Bars are in the image above.

For each element where you can make a change there will be a secondary dropdown menu like the one you can see above for Axes.

The More Options choice will open a formatting task pane for that element that gives even more choices, but the dropdowns usually work for adding or removing an element.

To give you a few examples of what you can do here:

I will often add a Data Table with Legend Keys to my charts so that I can see a table of the actual data below the chart. When I do this, I also make sure to set the Legend to None because the information is already in the data table since it includes legend keys.

Also, for pie charts I usually want to include the Data Labels and I usually do so at the Outside End so that I can see what value is represented by each slice in the pie. I also often change the data labels so they display percentages instead of values. I do so using the task pane label options:

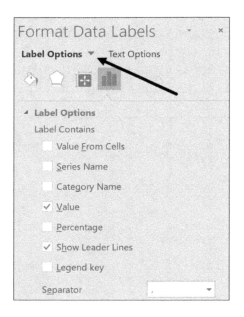

The Formatting Task Panes

To open the formatting task panes, you have a number of choices. You can click on More Options for any of the secondary element dropdown menus. Or you can right-click on your chart and choose the Format X option from the dropdown menu where X will be something like Data Labels, Data Series, Chart Area, Chart Title, etc. It all depends on where you're clicked on at the time.

No matter how you get there, once you have the task pane open you can move around to other formatting options for that chart or slide.

To do so, change the dropdown under the name of the task pane to what you need and then poke around to find where the particular formatting option you want is located.

So above where I wanted percentages to show instead of actual values, I had to choose "Series Sales Data Labels" from the dropdown menu and then click over to the Label Options image at the end of the four available icons.

Once there I could then check and uncheck what data to display for each pie slice.

If the task pane is already open you should be able to click onto your chart where you want to make your edit and the task pane should update to show formatting options for that part of the chart. But sometimes there's more than one option it could display, so that will get you close to what you need, but may not always get you exactly what you need.

As I mentioned, I use the task pane to change my pie chart labels to percentages. I also use it to "explode" a pie chart so that the individual slices have distance between them. And to rotate a pie chart so that the slices in the chart are where they look best visually.

Custom Colors

The color formatting we've covered so far is all quick hits. Pick a style, change colors from a pre-defined list of choices, etc.

But you can also change the colors or effects for any item in your chart to anything you want. You do this using the Shape Fill, Shape Outline, and Shape Effects choices available in the Chart Tools Format tab.

Both Shape Fill and Shape Outline will have dropdown menus that show sixty theme colors chosen to work with your theme and the ten standard colors, but you can always choose the More Colors option to use a different color.

For pie chart slices, bar charts, and column charts you should click on a segment and then choose a color from the Shape Fill dropdown.

In column and bar charts all segments for that particular data should be selected when you click on one of them. So here, for example, both of the Series 1 columns were automatically selected when I clicked on the left-hand column. You can see the circles at each corner that show they're currently selected.

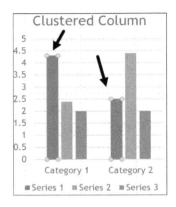

Once you're sure that the segment you want to change has been selected (and nothing else has), then you can pick your color from the Shape Fill dropdown.

For Line and Scatter charts, you have to use the Shape Outline dropdown menu instead.

You can also change your fill colors using the formatting task pane.

Filter Your Results

Click on your chart and you will see what looks like a little funnel off to the side. This is the Chart Filters option and will let you choose which data points appear in your chart if you don't want all of your data to display.

Format Chart Title and Other Text

To format text within a chart you can just select it like normal text and then use the text formatting options in the Font section of the Home tab. Just click into that text box and then make your formatting choices.

Resize A Chart

To resize a chart, you can click on the white boxes in the corners or on the sides and drag to the desired size.

You can also specify an exact size in the Size section of the Chart Tools Format tab.

Or you can go to the Format Chart Area task pane and in the Size & Properties section under Chart Options click on the Size arrow and then specify your values there.

The Format Chart Area pane also includes an option for specifying the exact position of your chart on your slide under the Position option in that same section.

Your other option is to click and drag the chart into position instead, but if you have multiple slides with charts on them this could create some disjointedness between slides as the charts appear to jump around from slide to slide.

If you have multiple charts on the same slide you can align them by dragging them into position. Dotted red lines will appear when the charts are aligned with one another.

Resize Chart Elements

When you resize a chart, all of the elements within the chart will also resize. So the title, the legend, the chart itself, will all adjust so that everything still fits nicely. But you can also resize just one chart element by clicking on it until you see it surrounded by a box with circles in the corners and then clicking and dragging on one of those circles.

Move Chart Elements

You can also move chart elements around. Once you've selected a specific chart element, like the chart title, you can left-click and drag to relocate it. Just be sure you're clicked onto a chart element and not the entire chart or you'll move the entire chart instead. Also, not all elements can be moved on their own. Titles and legends, yes. Axis labels, no.

* * *

Okay. Hopefully that gave you a solid overview on working with charts in PowerPoint. As I mentioned before, it's all based on how you'd work with charts in Excel, so if there's ever anything you can't figure out how to do when searching for help in PowerPoint also check Excel's help. And if you're familiar with charts in Excel you should be fine working in PowerPoint and vice versa.

Now on to SmartArt, which is like charts on steroids.

SmartArt

At its best SmartArt allows you to elevate a presentation to another level through the use of slick visual imagery. At its worst SmartArt creates confusion and looks pretentious.

So use it with care and consideration.

One of the biggest mistakes I see with using SmartArt is failing to understand that the graphic in question has a directionality to it or a flow to the numbers.

For example, there is a basic pyramid that you can insert using SmartArt. PowerPoint says you should use this pyramid "to show proportional, interconnected, or hierarchical relationships with the largest component on the bottom and narrowing up."

But I have seen this image used to show non-related values on the same slide. I've also seen it used where the largest value was on the top in the smallest segment.

And I've also seen where the first two levels of the pyramid were one related set of numbers and the third level was a completely different number.

Do not do that.

Only use SmartArt when the visual representation helps others to understand the point you're trying to make. If it doesn't do that, find a different way to present your information.

Okay. Now that the lecture is over, let's cover how you actually insert SmartArt into a presentation.

Insert SmartArt

One option is to click onto your slide and then go to the Illustrations section of the Insert tab and click on SmartArt.

This will bring up the Choose a SmartArt Graphic dialogue box:

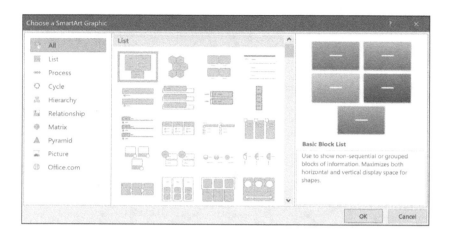

Another option is to use a content-type slide and click on the Insert a SmartArt Graphic image in the top row of choices. (It's the one with a bright-green two-dimensional arrow behind a text box.)

A third option, if you already have your text listed on your slide, is to select your text and then go to the Paragraph section of the Home tab, click on the Convert to SmartArt dropdown arrow, and then choose the SmartArt option you want from there.

(I'd usually recommend against that last option because chances are you didn't list your information in the order or format that will work with the SmartArt graphic you want to use and you're probably just better off creating the graphic from scratch. But it's there as an option if you want to try it.)

Choose and Insert Your SmartArt Graphic

Okay. So let's say you used the Insert tab and chose SmartArt under the Illustrations section and now you have the Choose a SmartArt Graphic dialogue box showing.

On the left-hand side of the dialogue box are the categories of SmartArt. There are graphics for lists, processes, cycles, hierarchies, relationships, matrices, and pyramids. There is also a section for pictures where you can incorporate a picture into a SmartArt graphic with additional analysis or comment boxes around that picture. The final category, Office.com, includes a few additional options.

As you click on each category there will be a number of possible options displayed in the center of the dialogue box.

Click on one of those options and you will see on the right-hand side of the dialogue box a sample of the graphic and a description of what it should be used for, like here for a basic pyramid:

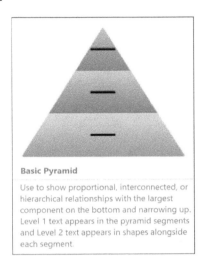

To select that option, click on OK in the bottom right corner of the dialogue box.

PowerPoint will then insert a template of that SmartArt graphic into your presentation. If you're using a theme, the colors used for the SmartArt graphic should match the theme you're using.

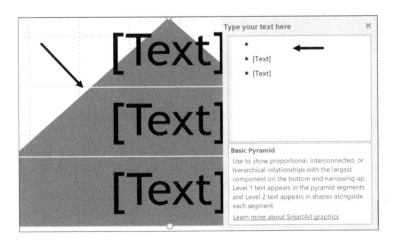

Add Your Text

At the same time that PowerPoint inserts your SmartArt graphic it should also open a Type Your Text Here dialogue box that shows sample text. (Like above where there are three bulleted points.)

Click into that dialogue box and replace the Text entries with your own values. This will overwrite the [Text] fields in the graphic like here where I replaced the three bullet points that said Text with Buyers, Prospects, and Potential Audience.

If that dialogue box isn't visible, you can just click onto the [Text] entries in the image itself and edit them there as well.

If you have a lot of text, though, it's easier to edit it in the dialogue box. To open that dialogue box when it isn't currently available, click on Text Pane in the Create Graphic section of the SmartArt Tools Design tab. This is especially true of situations where you want to add or delete additional entries.

To add an additional entry, just hit Enter on the last line of text. You should see another bullet point appear and you can just type in your text and a new element will be added to your graphic with that text.

Format Text and Elements

As you add or remove entries, the text should resize for you, but sometimes it doesn't resize enough for me like above with Buyers which is too big to fit on the interior of that section of the pyramid. Also, I sometimes find that I want to change the default font color or the fill color.

For example, above I don't like the black text on a dark background and I also don't like having each layer the exact same color. I think it would look better if each layer were a separate color.

To edit the text you can use the Font section of the Home tab just like you would for any other text entry. Use Ctrl + A to select all of the text at once if you want to change all of your text or select all of the text in an individual entry to change just that one entry.

To change the fill color of the elements in your graphic, the easiest way is to go to the SmartArt Tools Design tab and use the Change Colors dropdown menu. It has a number of pre-styled choices that use your theme colors.

For me that didn't work here because I wanted the bottom of the pyramid to be the darkest color and they didn't have an option for that. So instead I went to the SmartArt Tools Format tab and choose a different Shape Fill color for each of my elements.

As long as you choose your colors from the same Theme Colors column they will be complementary to one another.

The Format Shape text pane also allows you to change your Shape Fill. You can open it by right-clicking on the graphic and choosing Format Shape.

After I made my changes, here's what I ended up with:

Not perfect. I don't like where the placement of Buyers is in that top section and I had to go with a slightly darker fill there to keep using white text throughout, but I think it looks much better than the default that had black text and just one color for all of the segments.

Change SmartArt Graphic

That's much better, but I think if I were using this for an actual presentation I'd want to use a different graphic. One option is a reverse pyramid, like this:

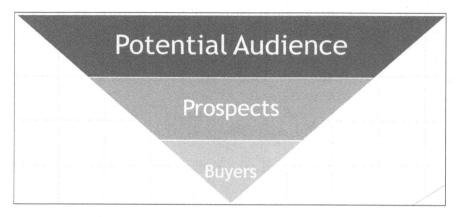

But I actually think that a process flow graphic is the better choice here. Something like this:

I lose the size component, but it does a better job of showing how you move from a potential audience to prospects to buyers.

To change your SmartArt graphic, click on the existing graphic and then go to the SmartArt Tools Design tab and choose a new option from the Layouts section. You can expand the entire section and click on More Layouts at the bottom if you need to move from one category of graphic to another like I did above.

I'd recommend that you do this immediately and not when you've done a lot of additional formatting because when you change your graphic it will reset to the original fonts, element fill colors, etc. So the images you see above are after I redid the changed font color, font size, and fill color. It didn't carry over. Also, I had to move around my text for both compared to the original.

SmartArt Effects

Another option you have is SmartArt Effects. For example, you can give a three-dimensional appearance or even directionality to some of the images.

The easiest way to do this is using the SmartArt Styles in the SmartArt Tools Design tab. Be careful, because that will overwrite any fill colors you've applied so if you're going to use one apply it first and then adjust your fill colors.

You can also use the Shape Effects dropdown in the Smart Art Tools Format tab. Be sure with this one to select all of your segments before you apply your effect or it will just apply to one element at at time.

Here I applied a SmartArt Style called Brick Scene to my process flow and then used Change Colors to apply different colors to each chevron:

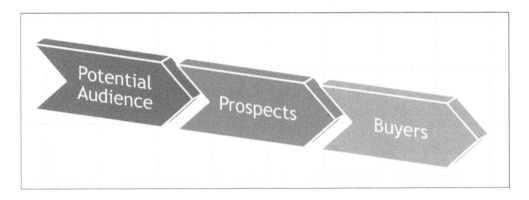

Notice that this is now three-dimensional and has more directionality to it than the original graphic did.

A Few More Options

There are a few more options for what you can do with SmartArt graphics to edit them. Let me walk through those real quick.

Convert To Text

In the Reset section of the Design tab you have an option to Convert To Text which will take your SmartArt graphic and turn it into text entries. This can be useful when you have a lot of text edits to make, but it does mean you will have to start over with the formatting of your graphic if you change it back to SmartArt.

Reset SmartArt

To reset the graphic back to the default settings that were in place when you inserted it you can use Reset Graphic from the Reset section of the SmartArt Tools Design tab. This will remove any color changes or effects you've added.

Move Up/Move Down

If you want to change the order of the components in your graphic, you can use the Move Up and Move Down options in the Create Graphic section of the SmartArt Tools Design tab.

That will move whichever segment you're clicked onto one segment forward or backward in the hierarchy. (If it's a pyramid it will actually move it up or down. If it's a process flow like we looked at above it will move it left or right.)

Change Direction

Clicking on Right To Left in the Create Graphic section of the SmartArt Tools Design tab will change the direction of any arrows in your graphic.

Demote/Promote

If you want to keep the information from one of your steps in your slide, but have it turned into a bullet point instead, you can click on it and then use the Demote option in the Create Graphic section of the SmartArt Tools Design tab.

To turn bulleted text into an element in your graphic, select the text and then click on Promote in that same section.

This is also a short-cut way to add additional items to your graphic. So, for example, I was able to demote one of my steps to a bullet point, then hit enter to get another bullet point, type in the text for that new bullet point, and then Promote both of the bullet points back into the graphic.

Add or Change Shapes

You are not stuck with the default shapes that are used in the SmartArt Graphic you choose. To change the shape for all of your elements at once, use Ctrl + A to select all of them and then go to the Shapes section of the SmartArt Tools Format tab under Change Shape and choose a different shape.

You can do the same for each individual element as well.

To move around the shapes in your graphic, select them and then click and drag them to where you want them.

You can also use shapes to add more elements to your graphic. Simply click on Add Shape in the top left corner of the Create Graphic section of the Design tab. That will add another element immediately after the element you currently have selected. Then you just have to right-click on the new element, choose Edit Text, and type in your new text.

Here is an example where I've changed the shape of my chevron process flow elements, added two new levels to the graphic, and also moved the elements around to create more of a downward flow from one step to the next:

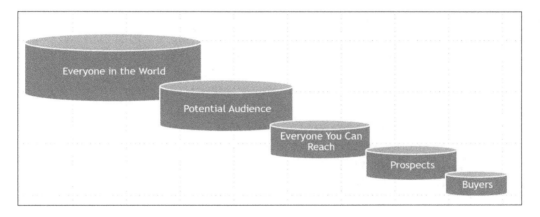

You can also copy any element and paste it back into the graphic to add another level.

Basically, if you have a vision for what you want to create, you can probably do it with SmartArt. Just remember that absolute power corrupts absolutely...

Avoid Confusion

At this point I feel obligated to remind you yet again that graphics in a presentation should be there to assist you in delivering your message but you need to be careful that they don't distract from that message.

Someone should be able to look at a SmartArt graphic in your presentation and just with a glance understand what you're trying to convey.

They shouldn't have to sit there and puzzle out why that graphic was used with that information.

For example, in the image below I've changed the last item to Cost of Production from Buyers. So now it flows from Potential Audience to Prospects to Cost of Production:

If I saw this image on a screen, you could be saying whatever you wanted, I'd be off on a mental tangent trying to figure out how you have a process flow that goes from Potential Audience to Prospects to Cost of Production.

Isn't Cost of Production part of a different flow? Doesn't that need to be with other finance-related fields? Why is it with potential audience?

Same issue if those arrows there on the chevrons were reversed. How do buyers flow to prospects? Huh.

Or if with the pyramids we had the buyers as the biggest layer. Shouldn't the potential audience be bigger than those who actually buy?

Use a bad graphic, you will lose your audience.

(I know, I'm just a stick in the mud. But remember, most of your bosses and clients probably are, too.)

* * *

Anyway. Enough of my forcing my opinions on you. But just think of all the time and energy that could be saved if we were all spared bad presentations.

Ah, that world would be amazing, wouldn't it?

Okay, then. Now on to Videos.

Videos

Insert Video is one of the options you have in your content slide defaults. It's in the bottom row and is an image of a strip of film. Click on that to bring up the Insert Video dialogue box which will let you navigate to the location on your computer where your video file is stored.

You can also insert a video using the Video dropdown in the Media section of the Insert tab. That allows you to choose between inserting a video that is stored on your device or one that is available online.

Choosing to insert a video from your device will open a navigation dialogue box. Choosing an online video will open a dialogue box where you can paste in the website address for that video. According to the Help documentation, PowerPoint 2019 supports videos from YouTube and Vimeo and requires use of Internet Explorer 11.

Also, since online videos play directly from those websites, they will only work if you have internet access and will be governed by the playback controls of those sites.

Finally, as the reminder in the bottom left corner of the dialogue box for inserting an online video says, "your use of online videos is subject to each provider's Terms of Use and Privacy Policy." Remember, there is such a thing as copyright and using someone else's material without valid permissions can be a costly mistake.

I'd generally advise that you try to use your own videos as much as possible to avoid any potential issues of that nature.

Okay, then. Whichever option you choose, find the video you want and insert it into your presentation by clicking on OK. Once you do so you should then see a still image from the video.

Hold your mouse over the video and you should see play buttons below it.

Play Video

Click on the play button on the left-hand side to play the video. When your video is playing that button will then turn to a pause button which you can click on if you need to pause the video.

There are also volume controls, a time counter, and the ability to move forward or backward in small increments (.25 seconds at a time).

When you navigate away from the slide with the video on it and come back to it, you may not see the play button below the video. If that happens simply move your mouse over the image to make it reappear.

During a presentation the play bar will appear as part of the bottom edge of the image instead of below it.

Change Video Screenshot

You can resize the video by clicking on it and then left-clicking and dragging on the white boxes along the perimeter. Use the white boxes in the corners to resize the image proportionately. Or you can use the Size section of the Video Tools Format tab. This will change the image proportionately.

Another option is to right-click on the video and choose Format Video from the dropdown to bring up the Format Video task pane. The Size section under Size & Properties will allow you to change the image size.

Video Tools Format Tab

Most video formatting options are limited to your own videos and will not work with the online videos, at least during replay.

The Video Styles section of the Video Tools Format tab lets you place borders or other effects around the video.

You can also apply a shape to your video using the Video Shape dropdown in that same section. If you do so, your video will play within a circle or arrow, etc.

The Adjust section has options where you can fix the brightness/contrast in the video, recolor it, or add a poster frame around the edges. Each dropdown menu shows a thumbnail of the available options.

Video Tools Playback Tab

In the Video Options section of the Video Tools Playback tab you have the choice of having the video play in automatically when the slide is presented, only when clicked upon, or in a designated order based upon when the other items in the slide appear.

You can also set the video to play full screen, loop until it's stopped, hide while not playing, or rewind after playing.

You can also control the volume, so for example if you wanted to mute the video, you could. Your sound options are low, medium, high, and mute. This would be separate from the computer's overall volume settings.

The Caption Options section allows you to link to a caption file for the video to allow for accessibility.

And the Editing section has options for trimming the video so that only a portion plays or adding a fade in or fade out.

Delete A Video

To delete the video, just click on it and then use the Delete key.

* * *

Alright. That's the basics of videos. One final caution about using your own videos in a presentation. If you insert your own video this will embed the video into your presentation which will substantially increase the file size.

Also, if you then distribute the presentation to others you could lose control over the video. (You will still own the copyright, but people are not always good about honoring that.)

But the biggest issue with using videos is having a quality video to begin with. No matter how much I wish it could, PowerPoint can't fix poorly shot, unedited videos of your dog.

Okay then. On to online pictures, 3D models, and icons.

Online Pictures, 3D Models, and Icons

The other three options that you have on a basic content slide are to insert online pictures, icons, and 3D Models.

Online Pictures

When using online pictures this means you're using someone else's image so I will remind you that copyright issues and trademark issues can be incredibly costly if you misstep. When you click on this option and then click on a category of images, you will see that there is a Creative Commons Only checkbox that is checked at the top.

I would recommend that you do not uncheck that box. Because if those photos are legitimately available under a creative commons license, then you are in fact free to use them. (Keep in mind that sometimes people steal an image and then upload it and indicate it is free to use, but they weren't the original creator so they can't do that, so as with all things online, proceed with caution. The bigger the audience for your presentation, the more you risk.)

You can also access the Online Pictures option using the Images section of the Insert tab. Choose Online Pictures from there.

Clicking on either option will bring up a web-based dialogue box that allows you to either search Bing or to find an image in your OneDrive account.

The dialogue box contains a series of categories you can click on or you can use the search bar to perform a keyword-based search for what you want.

Once you've performed a basic search or clicked onto a category there will be a small funnel located above the images and just below the search box. Click on that to specify the image size, type, layout, and color you want.

If you see an image you want to use, click on it, and then choose Insert from the bottom corner of the dialogue box and it will be inserted into your presentation.

Once the image is in your presentation you can use the Picture Tools Format tab to edit the image as needed.

3D Models

PowerPoint 2019 also allows you to insert 3D Models into your presentation. These models take an image in 3D and let you rotate the image to see all angles.

3D Models can be great for something like a chemistry class where you need to visualize what a certain molecule actually looks like. And I know something like this would've helped a few friends during geometry class. But I'd also warn that something like this can be seen as gimmicky if used for the wrong audience.

To insert one, either click on the 3D Models option in a content slide or go to the Illustrations section of the Insert tab and click on the dropdown arrow under 3D Models.

If you have your own model you'll need to use the dropdown and choose This Device.

If you don't have your own model choose Stock 3D Models from the dropdown or use the content slide option. This will open a web-linked dialogue box that shows a variety of categories you can choose from such as emojis, chemistry, anatomy, clothing, furniture, industrial, etc. You can also do a keyword search using the search box up top.

(It appears that these 3D models are generated by Microsoft so it is likely you won't have any copyright issue using them in a presentation. (And they seem to actively encourage users to modify and create their own 3D images.) However, if I were going to present to a very large audience or worked for a large company, I would still double-check that I had permissions to use these models first.)

Once you've found a model you want to use, click on it and then click on Insert at the bottom of the dialogue box which will place the model into your presentation.

Once you've inserted a 3D model into your slide, it will have a circular image on top with looping lines in two circles, one up and down and one side to side. Click on that image, hold the click, and move your cursor to rotate the image.

When you click on the model there will also be a 3D Model Tools Format tab that you can access that lets you reset the model to its original position, choose a specific model view, change the positioning of the model on the page, or change its size.

Icons

Icons are your final option for what you can insert from a content slide. They are basically little images that are like fancy line drawings of various subjects.

If you've ever seen the little man and woman images on a bathroom sign somewhere you know what an icon is.

You can insert an icon into your presentation by either clicking on the bird with a leaf image in the bottom right of the second row of choices on a slide or by using the Icons option in the Illustrations section of the Insert tab.

Clicking on either choice will open a web-linked Insert Icons dialogue box where you can search or choose icons from a variety of categories such as accessibility, analytics, animals, apparel, arrows, arts, etc.

Once more it appears these are ones designed by Microsoft so they should be fine for use in a presentation. But if you use them commercially in some way you may get into trouble, so once more consider consulting with a lawyer if you have big money to lose or high visibility.

(A presentation for your high school class of ten should be fine. One for a Fortune 100 company's annual report? Eh…Double-check. Both would be equally problematic if there is a problem, but one is much more likely to be noticed than the other.)

To insert an icon into your presentation, click on it, and then click on Insert.

Icons are smaller than the other items you can insert into a presentation, but you can resize them just like anything else.

Once inserted, you can click on your icon to see the Graphic Tools Format tab which will let you change the fill, outline, or effects of the icon just like you would with any shape.

Use Graphics Fill to change the color of your icon. Your default choices in the dropdown should match the theme you're using.

Master Slides: Just a Quick Note

Alright…

So we just covered a number of items you can insert into a presentation.

Now we need to talk about master slides. I mentioned them before in the context of editing the placement of your footer fields in your presentation. If you have a theme you like but the footers aren't where you want them, this is the best place to make that change.

But messing with your master slides can be dangerous because it impacts that entire template, so it's not something to do lightly. (And if it's a corporate template probably not something you should do at all.)

I would also recommend that if you're going to make changes to the master slides that you do so before you start to build your presentation. Otherwise you may have text that isn't fully visible or situations where some images or backgrounds update to show the changes you made and others don't.

Now that the warnings are out of the way, to see your master slides go to the Master Views section of the View tab, and click on the Slide Master option.

This will take you to the master slide for the type of content slide you were on at the time you made that selection.

If you look in the left-hand navigation pane you'll also see thumbnails for all master slides that are part of the theme. Remember all those layouts we walked through in *PowerPoint 2019 Beginner?* That's what those thumbnails are, one per layout.

To apply a change to just that slide layout, you can edit the slide you're on. But chances are you'll want to apply that change to all of the slide layouts. To do that, click on the very top thumbnail image in the left-hand pane instead. It should be offset to the left of the other slides in the task pane.

Any change you make to this master master slide will carry through to all the other slides that are listed below it.

For example, if you rearrange the position of your footer elements in this slide you should see that those footer elements also change in all of the other slides layouts.

When you click on that slide it will appear in your main workspace and you can click and drag the elements around just like you would with any slide. It's just that any changes you make here apply to every slide in your presentation.

Use the Background section of the Slide Master tab to change the overall appearance of your presentation. For example, you can use the Color dropdown menu there to change the color palette for your template to one of the twenty-plus color palettes that are shown or even to create a new color palette for the presentation.

(As you hold your mouse over each one the presentation should change in the background to let you see what it will look like.)

If you do change your master slides, I'd recommend that you Rename it using the Edit Master section so that you don't overwrite something you didn't intend to.

But, honestly, we're on the edge of advanced PowerPoint here so I'm not going to go into this in more detail, I just wanted you to know that the option existed in case you ever need it..

Select All

You can select all of your slides or all of the objects on a slide using the Select All option.

The easiest way to use Select All is through the control shortcut, Ctrl + A.

To select all of the text in a text box, click into the text box first.

To select all of the objects on a slide, click somewhere outside a text box first.

To select all of your slides, click on a slide thumbnail image in the left-hand navigation pane first.

For text the text will be highlighted in gray. For objects you'll see boxes around each shape/image. For slides you'll see a red border around each slide thumbnail image in the navigation pane.

Another option for selecting all is to go to the Editing section of the Home tab and then choose Select All or Select Objects from the dropdown menu.

Sections

It is possible to split a presentation into multiple sections. PowerPoint recommends doing this to allocate tasks between team members, for example. It also makes it easier to move slides around because you can collapse a section and then click and drag that whole section to a new location in the presentation.

If you have a very lengthy presentation it can also make navigating the presentation a lot easier if you use sections and collapse them. Like so:

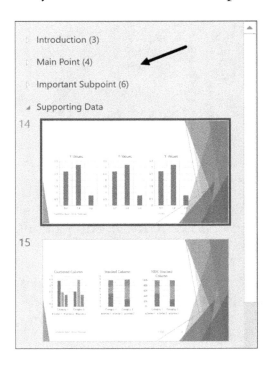

You can see that I have three sections that are collapsed (Introduction, Main Point, and Important Subpoint) before the current section called Supporting Data. There are thirteen slides in those other sections that I've hidden by collapsing the sections. (The number of slides in each section is in parens at the end of the section name.)

If I needed to see the three introductory slides I could do so by expanding that section. If all slides were visible I'd have to scroll up to see them and wouldn't also be able to see the thumbnails of the slides in my current section.

To insert a section, right-click onto the space in the left-hand navigation pane directly above the slide thumbnail where you want to start your new section and choose Add Section from the dropdown menu.

This will insert a new section starting with that slide. You should also see a dialogue box called Rename Section that shows a section name of Untitled Section. Type over that name to give the section the name you want to use.

If you don't change the section name immediately, you can always right-click on the name and choose Rename Section from the dropdown menu later to bring up that dialogue box.

Either way, click on Rename once you've entered your text.

There are other options available for sections once you've created one as you can see here, just right-click on the section name:

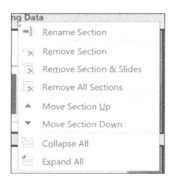

Remove Section will remove the section name but keep the slides. Remove Section & Slides will remove both. Remove All Sections will remove all section names but keep the slides.

Move Section Up or Move Section Down will move the entire section, including its slides. Collapse All will hide all slides but show the section names. Expand All will show all slides as well as section names.

These options are also available in the Slide section of the Home tab under the Section dropdown menu.

Comments

It is always a good idea when working on a draft document with others to keep any comments or questions out of the body of the document. In PowerPoint you can do this using Comments.

To insert a comment, go to the point in the presentation where you want to make the comment and either right-click and choose New Comment from the dropdown menu, or click onto that location and then go to the Comments section of the Review tab and choose New Comment.

This will open the Comments pane on the right-hand side of the workspace. Your user name will appear above a white text box. Type your comment there.

Once entered, each comment will show who made it and when.

On the presentation slide a comment is represented by a small quote bubble in a peach-sort of color.

Click to add title

Click on that comment bubble to open the Comments task pane and see the text of the comment. If comments aren't visible you can also go to the Show Comments dropdown in the Comments section of the Review tab and check the box next to Comments Pane.

Comments will not show when you have the presentation in slide show mode, but I'd recommend that if you do use comments that you delete them before the final version is saved.

To do this, go to the Comments section of the Review tab, click on the Delete dropdown, and choose Delete All Comments in This Presentation.

To navigate between comments in a presentation you can either use the Previous and Next options in the Comments section of the Review tab, or their icons which are located at the top of the Comments pane. Previous looks like a comment bubble with a left-hand arrow in the top corner. Next looks like a comment bubble with a right-hand arrow in the top corner.

To reply to an existing comment type into the white text box directly below the comment which says "Reply…" in gray letters.

You can also make a new comment instead, but that's the old way and a messier option that sometimes doesn't maintain the thread of the conversation.

To edit an existing comment, click on the text of the comment and it will become a white text box again where you can then add to, delete, or edit the text.

Incorporate Group Edits

Unlike Word, PowerPoint does not have a track changes option. What they recommend doing instead is to save the original draft of your presentation and then save a renamed version of the presentation and make that renamed version available for people to add their comments or make their edits through a share site.

Once those edits or comments have been made to the second version of the presentation you can then bring them into the original version of the presentation and review them by using the Compare function.

I will note here that I personally think Compare is poorly-designed and do not use it myself, but I'm presenting it here so you know about it and how to use it.

So, having said that, to compare two presentations open the original version of the presentation in PowerPoint, go to the Compare section of the Review tab, and click on Compare.

This will open the Choose File to Merge with Current Presentation dialogue box. Navigate to where you have the second version of the presentation saved, select it, and then click on the Merge button.

You will now see your initial presentation with a Revisions pane on the right-hand side. For me it was a little small so I had to resize it by clicking along the edge and dragging to the left once I saw the two-sided arrow.

If there are no edits to the current slide it will tell you so and then tell you the next slide which does have edits. Like this:

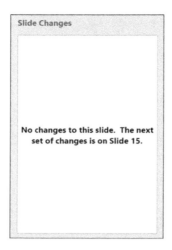

If there are comments in the merged presentation you will see the Comments pane on the right-hand side as well. If there are no comments in the current slide it will say so but there will be previous and next navigation options to move to the next comment in the presentation.

For changes that were made to the presentation itself you can either navigate to the specified slide using the thumbnails in the navigation pane on the left-hand side of the screen or go to the Compare section of the Review tab and use the Next option.

(The Previous option will take you to any prior edits if you're in the middle of the presentation.)

This is also where you can open or close the Reviewing Pane.

Now, here's where it gets weird. It's all backwards how this works in my opinion. Because if someone has made edits to a presentation I want to see how it looks with those edits incorporated. But the default for Compare is to show the original presentation as it was before any edits were made.

The view of the current slide as you see it on the screen is how it existed in your original version. To see how it looks with the identified edits, click on the small image showing a piece of paper with a pencil in the top right corner of the slide. That will then show a description of the edit(s). Click on the box next to each edit description to then show the edit on the slide.

To remove the edit from your view, uncheck that box.

This is the strangest part: You can only accept an edit when the change is *not* visible on the slide.

You do this by either going to the Compare section of the Review tab, clicking on the Accept dropdown option, and then choosing Accept Change or by right-clicking on the little pencil with paper and choosing Accept Change from there.

Once you accept that change (that you couldn't see as you were accepting it), the change will then appear on the slide.

(Who came up with that, I do not know.)

At least they did set it up so that when a change is visible, you can reject it, which you do by going to the Compare section of the Review tab or by right-clicking and choosing the Reject option.

For changes that involve moving a slide to a new location or deleting a slide or a section, those will be flagged in the left-hand navigation pane, separate from changes that were made to an individual slide's content or format.

Honestly, I find this a very awkward way to review changes in a presentation. If I were faced with a situation like this what I would likely do, assuming I trusted my team not to make crazy edits that I needed to know about, would be to immediately accept all of the changes in the presentation and then review the presentation as if it was supposed to be a final version. (Which is basically just reviewing the second version of the presentation without ever having to Compare the two versions.)

Compare is nice in the sense that it will keep you from missing any changes that were made that can slip by and will let you know who made that change, but it's really messy how they've set it up.

Zoom and Views

We've pretty much covered the big ticket items you need to know to work at an intermediate level in PowerPoint, but I wanted to cover a few little clean up items before we wrap up.

First, let's look at how to use Zoom and what the different Views options are.

Zoom

On occasion, you may want to increase the size of the slide you're viewing or you may want to decrease its size. This can be done using Zoom.

The easiest way to do this is to use the slider in the bottom right corner of PowerPoint. You'll see a negative sign, a line with a midpoint marked and a rectangle perpendicular to that line, and then a plus sign and a percentage value.

Click on the rectangle to drag to the desired zoom level or click on the line on either side of the rectangle to move in the desired direction. By default I tend to have my slides around 85-90% which makes each slide fully visible on my screen.

You can also click on the plus and minus marks at either end of the line to move up or down to the nearest 10% mark. So originally you'll move from 85% to 80% or 90% but then you'll move to 70% or 100% and so on.

If you resize the PowerPoint window to be less than the full screen this may require you to adjust your zoom level to still see your full slide.

Your other option is to go to the Zoom section of the View tab and click on Zoom. This will bring up the Zoom dialogue box. You can type a percentage value into the Percent box or use the up and down arrows there to change the value. Or you can click into one of the white circles to select a pre-listed value. Your choices are Fit, 400%, 200%, 100%, 66%, 50%, and 33%.

Choosing a value that is greater than your current value will make the slide on your screen larger. Choosing a value that is less than your current value will make it smaller. The panes on either side will not change size, just the main workspace.

Click OK to actually apply your zoom level.

If you zoom to the point where you can't see the entire slide then scroll bars will appear on the bottom and right side of the slide image so that you can scroll to see the entire slide.

You can return your slide to a size that will fit the available space by clicking on Fit to Window in the Zoom section of the View tab or by choosing Fit in the dialogue box.

Views

Normal View

You can also change your default slide view if you want. This is done by selecting one of the options in the Presentation Views section of the View tab.

The default, or Normal, view shows the one slide that you're currently on in the center of the screen with a navigation pane on the left-hand side that contains thumbnails of the other slides in your presentation. If you have notes on your presentation, those will appear at the bottom.

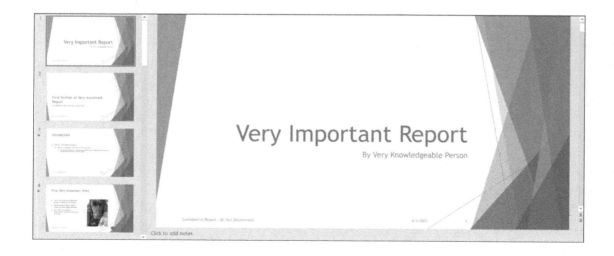

Outline View

Outline View, the next option, replaces the thumbnails in the presentation with the text from each slide shown in a bulleted or list format. You can click on that text and delete, edit, or add to it but not format it. In this view, the current presentation slide is still visible on the right half of the screen, but it's smaller and the notes section below the slide remains.

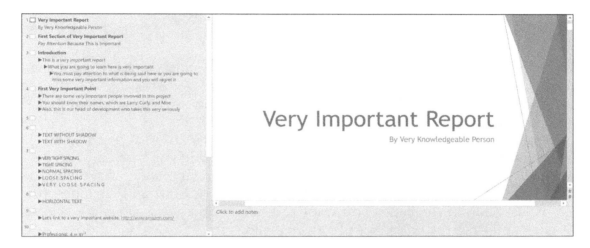

This view is good for quickly reviewing or editing the text in your presentation, but it's not going to show you images or layout in that section.

According to PowerPoint "[w]orking in Outline view is particularly handy if you want to make global edits, get an overview of your presentation, change the sequence of bullets or slides, or apply formatting changes."

Slide Sorter

The Slide Sorter view shows you thumbnails of all of your slides but no central slide to edit.

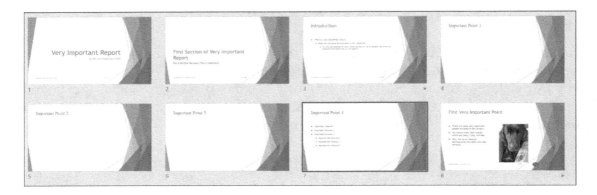

This is probably the most useful view for moving slides around within your presentation. The big advantage of this view over the Normal view is that you have more slides visible. Combine this view with Zoom Out and you can see approximately seventy slides at once.

To move a slide, left-click and drag it to where you want it. When you do this, all other slides will move over to accommodate the slide you moved.

You can also select multiple slides by clicking on one slide and then either holding down Ctrl and clicking on individual slides or Shift and clicking on the first or last slide in the series you want to select. Once your slides are selected, left-click and drag the entire set of selected slides to their new location.

Rather than click and drag the slides you can also use Copy (Ctrl +C) or Cut (Ctrl + X) and Paste (Ctrl + V) to move the slides around.

Notes Page

The next view, the Notes Page view, will show you the slide and any notes for that slide as they will appear when printed. You can actually click into the text box for the notes in this view and add or edit your notes.

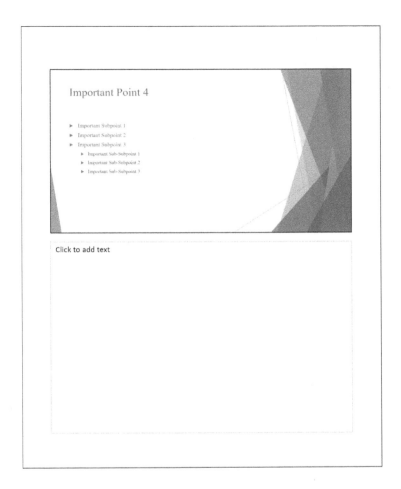

(If all you want is to know what notes you have on a slide, the easier option is to stay in the Normal view and just click on Notes in the status bar at the bottom of the screen. Click on Notes again to hide your notes from view.)

Reading View

The final view, the Reading View, shows you how the slide will look as part of a presentation, including any animations and transitions, without requiring that you view it as a full screen presentation.

In this view, you can use the arrows in the status bar at the bottom to move forward or backward through the presentation. You can also just click on the slide or use the arrow keys on your keyboard to move forward

Use Esc or left-click on Menu (which is between the two arrows in the status bar) and choose End Show to get back to the normal PowerPoint screen. You can also click on the Normal icon in the status bar next to the right arrow to get back to the Normal View.

Save As PDF

I covered how to save a file and how to change the format of that file when you save it in *PowerPoint 2019 Beginner*, but there are a few extra tips I wanted to share about saving a PowerPoint presentation as a PDF.

To save a PowerPoint presentation as a PDF file choose the Save As option.

Next, choose the location where you want to save the file. This will bring up the Save As dialogue box which includes a Save As Type dropdown menu at the bottom.

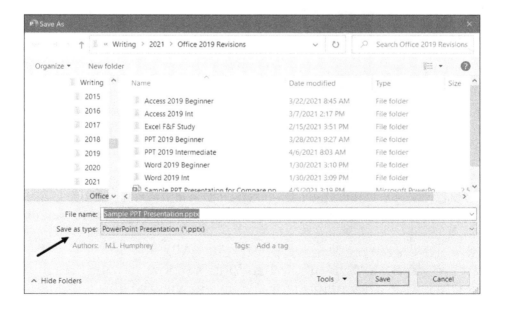

Click on the arrow for that dropdown menu and choose PDF, which is the fourth option down. Once you do this a box that says Options will appear below that dropdown menu. Click on it to see additional options related to PDF files.

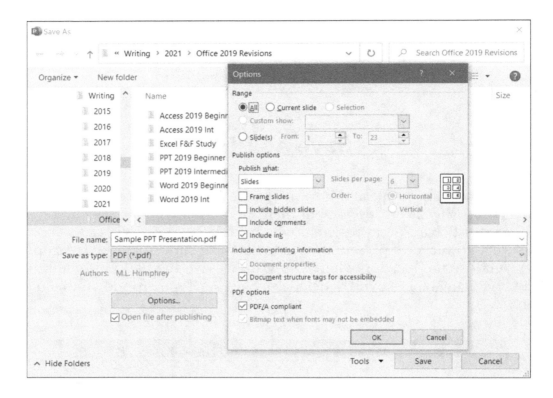

If you just want only the current slide to be saved as a PDF, click on Current Slide in the first row of options under Range.

If you want to save a set of slides but not the entire presentation as a PDF, use the Slide(s) option in the Range section and then type in the first slide number and last slide number for your range of slides.

If the slides you want to save are not continuous, then select them first using Ctrl and the navigation pane and then when you choose to Save As a PDF, use the Selection choice from the Range section. This will save your selected slides as a single PDF file.

Otherwise, just leave the Range option set to All.

You can also create a PDF of the handouts version of your presentation, the notes pages from the presentation, or the outline view of the presentation using the Publish What dropdown in the Publish Options section. Choosing handouts will let you specify the number of slides to include on each printed page.

The rest of the options can generally be left as-is unless you have a specific reason to change them.

Once you've made your selections click on OK and then click on Save to save your file as a PDF.

Another way to generate a PDF file of your presentation is by going to the File tab and using the Export option. From there you can choose to Create a PDF/XPS Document. It brings up a Publish as PDF or XPS dialogue box that looks the same as the Save As dialogue box except that the PDF file type is already selected and the Options button is over to the right.

Both approaches should give you a PDF file that meets your specifications.

Save As An Image

Another Save As option that I've used on occasion was the ability to save my presentation as images. This is because in the past I've used PowerPoint to create the images that I placed in my books. I would paste the screenshot I intended to use into a PowerPoint slide, add arrows and text, trim the image, and then export the result as a .jpg image I could insert into my presentation.

(As a side note, that's not the best way to do things, but it was the best way I knew how to do them at the time.)

Okay, so how do you do this?

To generate images of your PowerPoint slides, choose Save As, and then choose your location you want to save your file.

This will once more open the Save As dialogue box. This time you should choose GIF Graphics Interchange Format (*.gif), JPEG File Interchange Format (*.jpg), PNG Portable Network Graphics Format (*.png), or TIFF Tag Image File Format (*.tif) from the Save As Type dropdown menu.

Which image type you prefer is up to you. These days I tend to use the TIFF option, but there are places that will only accept a JPEG. For most uses it's really not going to make a difference, but if it does you have all the choices available.

Once you select an image file type and click on Save, PowerPoint is going to ask you, "Which slides do you want to export?"

If you choose All Slides it will create a new folder using the name you have the presentation saved under and will then save each individual slide as its own image file within that folder. It will name those files according to their slide number. So you'll have a folder named, for example, PowerPoint 2019 Intermediate with files inside it named Slide1, Slide2, etc.

If you choose Just This One instead, PowerPoint will save just the current slide as an image file using with the name of the presentation. So be careful there. You can think it saved it all as one file, but it didn't.

Slide Transitions

In *PowerPoint 2019 Beginner* I covered how to use animations to have only a portion of the text on a slide appear at a time. This can be very useful when doing a presentation so that the people you're talking to don't read ahead and stop listening to you.

I tend to have a strong dislike for most of the animations options where text spins onto the screen or wheels in or grows and turns, etc. It's usually not necessary and distracts from what you're trying to do.

Which is why I didn't cover the equivalent for slides, which are called Transitions. I'd generally recommend caution when using these.

I have seen them used effectively, however. I once attended a presentation on the psychology of evil that started with the presenter playing a timed presentation of images from a prisoner of war camp with some sort of sound effect each time the slide changed.

Five minutes of that drives the point home.

But in general? Approach with caution.

Okay, so how do you add transitions to slides?

Click on the slide in the left-hand pane that you want to transition to and then go to the Transitions tab and click on the transition type you want to use from the Transition To This Slide section.

As you click on your choice, PowerPoint will briefly show the transition in the main view portion of the screen. So you will see the prior slide transitioning to your current one using the selected transition type.

If you miss this demonstration or want to see it again, you can click on the Preview option on the left-hand side of the Transitions tab and it will run again.

If you want the transition to take more or less time, this can be adjusted in the

Timing section of the Transitions tab by changing the Duration.

If you want all of your slides to have the same transition settings that you've already applied to the current slide (duration, sound, type), click on Apply To All in the Timing section of the Transitions tab.

If you really want to annoy people, you can even add a sound to your slide transition. This is also under the Timing section of the Transitions tab. Choose the sound you want from the Sound dropdown. The sound will then play as the slide transitions. If you choose just a sound transition but no movement, you'll need to run the slide show or use the Reading View to hear it in action.

(And, again, I have seen sound transitions used effectively before, but not often. That *one* time is the only one I can remember.)

The Transitions tab is also where you can change the setting that advances a presentation to the next slide using a mouse click. That option is on by default.

You can instead set it to advance after a set period of time under the Advance Slide settings in the Timing section. This can be a good option for when you're using a series of images in a PowerPoint presentaiton as a background slide show on a computer screen while waiting to present, for example.

To see the timed transitions in action, you'll need to launch the slide show or use the Reading View.

And to apply the same timing to all of your slides, select them all first, and then specify the setting you want to use or check Apply to All when you're done.

Conclusion

Alright. That's it.

Hopefully you now have a better understanding of PowerPoint than you did when you started. However, as the name implies, this was not meant to be a comprehensive guide to PowerPoint. The basics of using PowerPoint were already covered in *PowerPoint 2019 Beginner* and there are some more advanced skills I didn't mention here at all or that I mentioned enough for you to know about but not in full and complete detail.

But at this point I hope you've learned enough about how PowerPoint works that you can find those additional answers on your own. PowerPoint, like all of Office, tends to follow a certain logic, so that when you don't know how to do something you can often figure it out based on how you did other similar tasks.

But there are also a number of excellent help options out there to assist you.

The first option is to go to the Help tab and click on Help, or use F1, to launch the PowerPoint Help task pane.

You will see some popular categories listed as well as a search box where you can type in what you're looking for. Using PowerPoint help will often lead you to the answer you need.

Within PowerPoint some of the menu choices also have a basic description which you can see if you just hold your mouse over them. In addition, some of those descriptions include a Tell Me More note at the bottom that you can click on to launch the specific help description for that option.

For example, if I go to the Text section of the Insert tab and hold my mouse over the WordArt dropdown it tells me that I can "add some artistic flair to my document using a WordArt text box" and then has Tell Me More at the bottom. If I click on that Tell Me More it takes me straight to the help section for Insert WordArt.

If the help options within PowerPoint are not enough, you can also do an internet search to find your answer. Be sure to include the version of PowerPoint you're working in and some keywords that are relevant to your search. I usually choose the support.office.com results first because I expect them to be the most official and reliable option. But if it's a "can you do this weird thing" question as opposed to a "how does this work" question, then sometimes you'll need to branch out to other sources.

Worst case scenario, there are a number of online user forums where you can ask a question.

Also, you're always welcome to reach out to me. Chances are I'll know the answer or be able to find it for you easily enough. Just send an email.

And that's that. Remember, the goal of a presentation is usually to convey information, so if whatever you're trying to do with your presentation doesn't accomplish that, then don't do it. PowerPoint is tremendously powerful and gives you all sorts of options, but that can be as dangerous as it is helpful. So keep it as clean and simple as you can. Don't let the appearance overwhelm the message.

Good luck with it.

INDEX

ABOUT THE AUTHOR

M.L. Humphrey is a former stockbroker with a degree in Economics from Stanford and an MBA from Wharton who has spent close to twenty years as a regulator and consultant in the financial services industry.

———————————————

You can reach M.L. at mlhumphreywriter@gmail.com or at mlhumphrey.com.